LEADER, NOT A BOSS

BENJAMIN BABIC

Copyright © 2023 Benjamin Babic
All rights reserved.

ISBN: 978-3-00-077434-8

To my mom, thank you for raising me into the person I am today and for always believing in me.

CONTENTS

INTRODUCTION 1

PART 1: THE BEGINNING

01
LEADERSHIP 11

02
THE POWER 16

03
MICROMANAGEMENT 21

04
MY LEADERSHIP RULES 25

PART 2: HIRE

01
HIRING FOR ATTITUDE AND POTENTIAL 41

02
TIPS FOR THE INTERVIEW 45

03
FAVORITE INTERVIEW QUESTIONS 48

PART 3: DEVELOP

01
YOUR TEAM MEMBERS 55

02
ONE-ON-ONE'S 63

03
FEEDBACK 66

03
COACHING 73

04
INDIVIDUAL DEVELOPMENT PLAN 76

05
PERFORMANCE IMPROVEMENT PLAN 82

06
ADDITIONAL TIPS DEVELOPMENT 84

PART 4: RETAIN

01
HOW TO KEEP EMPLOYEES MOTIVATED? 89

02
KEEP THE CHALLENGE HIGH 99

03
DON'T HOLD YOUR PEOPLE BACK 101

04
RECOGNISE 105

PART 5: LAY OFF

01
WHEN IS IT TIME? 113

02
HOW TO DO IT? 117

FINAL THOUGHTS 120
RESOURCES 124
ENDNOTES 125

INTRODUCTION

Being a manager does not just come with a fancy title, benefits, and higher salaries. Managerial positions come with many new responsibilities, and achieving targets and improving performance are not the biggest ones. A person stepping into a managerial position with direct reports has the biggest responsibility to their team. Being a people manager means you are not a single contributor anymore, and you need to deliver results through your team. In research conducted for HBR[i], results showed that 62% of people who gave their managers good grades are willing to go the extra mile. Imagine having a team of 10, and if 6 are willing to do more than is requested and go above average, the result for the company can be incredible. It is easy to conclude managers have considerable influence on their teams, not just on performance and job satisfaction, but also on mental health. As per Forbes[ii] article, 69% of people said their manager has the greatest impact on their mental health. Having a good manager means a lot, and you can feel the difference in almost all aspects of your life, not just professionally. Working with an understanding and supportive person who creates a healthy environment at work, where you are motivated to give your best, will for sure have a positive knock-on effect on other aspects of your life. The same goes if you have a bad manager. Having a bad manager has a negative effect on both professional and private life, and it can lead to employees leaving the companies just to escape that person. Research published in the DDI Frontline Leader Project[iii] shows that 57% of people who leave the company do so because of a bad manager, not the company itself. Bearing in mind all the above and those shocking numbers, it is more than evident what a huge influence a manager has. My best guess is most of you reading this book have experienced what it means to work with a bad and a good manager. In this book, I want to discuss my view on what makes a good manager and a leader in the hope of having more managers striving to have a positive impact.

You are wondering, who am I to talk to you about leadership, people management, and people development? Fair question. Let me give a bit of background. I started my career as a management trainee, and for two years, I was trained in how to be a manager. The whole experience was amazing; I even got to work in Japan for 6 months. Afterward, I took over my first managerial position and my first team. Throughout my whole managerial career, I was always leading big teams. Since I had my first position as a store manager with a team of 25 people and then to a team of 400, I am currently leading together with my 7 direct reports. I got to work with wonderful people, lead great teams, and face particularly challenging situations. I am grateful for every experience I had, good or bad, because I learned from it, and it brought me to the point where I am now.

Since the beginning of my people manager career, being aware of my impact on my team and indirectly on their communities, I have been striving to be a good manager. My wish was always to create a positive work environment where we all work hard and have an enjoyable time and fun. I never saw work just as a workplace. Since we spend so much time at work, the workspace becomes the second place we spend the most time at, and it must be joyful and fun. I always wanted to create a work environment where my team would come happy, motivated, and inspired to work, and without any "stomachache." I am very aware that the mood and energy of the place mostly come from me, and hence, I am always trying to be positive and spread good vibes. It is not always possible, and I am human with bad and good days, but I see it as my responsibility to be there for my team, even when I am feeling down. There is a saying, "The fish stinks from the head," and I agree with it—the manager sets the mood and energy in the team. I'm not saying work should be only fun; my point is that with a good mood and positive environment, performance also increases. I see my team as my primary responsibility, and they are the ones achieving targets and bringing in results. My role is to support them and help them do their best. With that being said, most of my time is spent working with my team. Over time, I've come to realize that the commitment to and prioritization of people's development varies among different managers. Irrespective of the organization you are employed in, if you have individuals under your supervision, your foremost responsibility should be to guide and foster their growth. I heard managers saying, "I couldn't do weekly meetings with my direct reports because I'm too busy," which is completely wrong. I know it's a strong statement, and many people won't agree with me, but those people are not in leadership and people management. Or they maybe are but shouldn't be. When you are a people manager, you are expected to deliver through your team, and your main task is supporting them. Most of your time should be spent working with your team. Hence, you need to have time for them, especially for meeting with your team members. Your success is measured by how successful your team is.

I worked for a company that had a strong customer focus; the customer was king. It was expected by every manager to take care of some of the customers personally. We discussed more about customers than our teams. I still remember the exercise we were doing where managers needed to put priorities for their positions, and among the choices were customers and employees. All my colleagues have put customers first place, and I was the only outcast putting employees in the first place. I always saw my primary task as being there for my team, making sure they were supported, engaged, and motivated. In return, they would then provide great service for the customers. Richard Branson, who I admire a lot, has the same view that he embodied in the whole Virgin Group. His famous quote, with which I could not agree more, goes:

"Clients do not come first. Employees come first. If you take care of your employees, they will take care of the clients."

— *Richard Branson*

My leadership style has evolved since I first started in a managerial position. I got my first team at the age of 26, and honestly, apart from having a bunch of training, I had no clue what I was doing. It was exceedingly difficult at the beginning. I inherited a team from an experienced and very likable manager. For my team, I was just a kid from college without any real work experience. That team had great individuals, but also one that was testing my limits. Those were the ones who tried to manipulate me (sometimes successfully), they tried to cheat (and sometimes succeeded), but they helped me evolve and learn. In the beginning, I avoided difficult discussions and confrontations. I tried to be nice to and please everyone, but that is not how it works. And people tried to take advantage. I learned the hard way that you need to protect good team members and take out the rotten fruit. Now, I do not want this to go in a negative direction, but I want to show you that I learned from my own mistakes. My wish is to point out the downfalls that I had so you could learn from them and avoid them in real life. So, lesson number one, before we even start—do not avoid confrontations and difficult discussions. You are just dragging the situation down, feeling uncomfortable and anxious while the overall performance of the team is suffering. Deal with individuals, give constructive feedback, and be decisive.

Not only challenging situations but also challenging individuals helped me grow. However, I was lucky enough to have many more wonderful team members, many of whom I am still in contact with, and I am thrilled to see their growth and development. Many amazing people helped me come to where I am now. I am lucky enough even to call some of them my friends.

I will never forget my closest collaborator at that time, my HR assistant working with me for almost two years. She is a person with a warm heart but can be strict and direct when needed. She went beyond to finish tasks, and she was a high performer, a person I could 100% trust. After holding a managerial position in another company, her wish was to step back and do something less stressful, which involved working with people. We were an awesome team. We jointly improved the engagement of the team and implemented many changes in the store, and I can say I had a true partner. What I appreciated the most was that I learned a lot from her. Even though she was my direct report, she never held back when she thought I was doing something wrong. She would take me aside and express her opinion. I valued her feedback greatly! Together, we navigated through the ramp-up of the operations, through the heights of COVID-19, and many other challenges. Till today, she remains one of the most valuable collaborators and team members I have had so far and a very dear friend.

WHY DID I WRITE THIS BOOK?

The inspiration to author the book came from my two former team members. During our conversation, they pointed out how relevant my leadership was to their development and how they were using the same development techniques with their direct reports. I realized I wanted to put together everything I learned from a leadership perspective on a paper in a wish to help other people as well. In addition, while I was doing my MBA, leadership was studied at a high level, with the practical level being disregarded. I was surrounded by amazing people—ambitious, motivated, eager to succeed and grow. Extremely fast, I realized I was among the rare participants who had the opportunity to manage a big team. Leadership skills are essential for any person wanting to advance in their careers. Regardless of the team size, a person climbing up the corporate ladder will have direct reports. Knowing how to lead and develop individuals and teams is crucial for success. Yet, the courses that are part of the curriculum in many study programs discuss leadership on a high level. In fact, most candidates who enroll in such study programs do not have people management/leadership experience but will need it later. This got me thinking about what I can do to support new managers facing the challenges of managing people.

WHO IS THIS BOOK FOR?

The book is written for young and rising managers. Many new managers finding themselves in a new position will have a lot of questions, a lot of uncertainties, and a lot of doubts. Trust me, I've been there and done that. This book is intended for people who are leading a team for the first time. Advice written in this book can help new managers develop their leadership style and grow as leaders more easily and sustainably.

HOW IS THE BOOK STRUCTURED?

The book is structured in a way that follows the different stages managers can find themselves in relation to their team members. It starts with a discussion about leadership and what I believe makes the difference between a leader and a manager. Even though the majority think those two terms are the same, they go hand in hand but are different. Afterward, the topic of hiring for your team will be discussed, with advice on how to prepare for the interview. You read correctly. Even though you will be the one conducting the interview, you still need to be prepared. The following section will be about the development of direct reports. You will have team members with different ambitions and career goals. How to approach those? What tools can help you? After the discussion about development, we will deal with employee retention. Having a team member who wants to leave your team can be difficult; I experienced it a few times. How you act in this situation is what defines you as a leader. The last part is unfortunate, but in business life, it is very necessary—how to let someone go. For most people, that is a real nightmare, and it is not easy. We will go through some tactics and preparations you can have to make those situations easier.

BE ADVISED

Different readers might be interested in different topics. Feel free to skip chapters and read first the one that makes the most sense for you. The book is written in a way that serves as an educational book, not a novel; hence, chapters can be read in the order you want. **Important note before moving on:** Would I say I know everything about leading people? Never. I have so much to learn and improve, and I am 100% aware of that. In this book, there are many examples of how I dealt with the situations. Would I say that is the best way? No. It is up to you to decide how you want to develop your leadership style. I want to explain the challenges I faced and the failures I made in my career to help you avoid them. In the end, it is your decision, and you should develop your own leadership style.

PART 1:
THE BEGINNING

01
LEADERSHIP

There is a tendency to confuse management and leadership and even think those terms mean the same. Well, not exactly. Manager is a specific role, while leadership is a skill. You can be a manager without being a leader, and you can be a leader without being a manager. The manager will ensure people follow the company rules and fulfill their tasks. On the other hand, a leader will make sure his employees are growing and are empowered to think for themselves to achieve the desired outcome. As per Julie Zhuo, author of The Making of a Manager, *leadership is someone's ability to guide and influence other people*. Hence, leadership is a quality more than a job, and anyone can be a leader in their own community.

In today's world, we are witnessing a phenomenon where being an influencer is a real job, and many people are making money out of it, for which I have utmost respect. These influencers have large communities of followers who buy products they use, and they go to hotels and restaurants suggested by influencers. Those influencers are leaders of their communities, as they can influence opinion and lead their followers. I used the most obvious example, but here, you can see that one can be a leader without having disciplinary authority over other people. However, in this book, I'm solely focusing on leaders who are in managerial positions, the leaders who have disciplinary authority and direct reports.

My management style has always been leading people rather than managing them. The question is, how do you come to a point where your direct reports are willing to follow you? Long gone are the times when direct reports blindly listened to managers and fulfilled all tasks they were given without any questions asked. That is the "boss" way of doing things that is just not working anymore. In today's world, you need to make sure that your people trust and are willing to follow you on a journey of growth. You need to be a leader, not a boss.

One of the first steps is to build teams around trust relationships and establish connections with them. That is always my first aim—I get to know my people, and I know who they are outside of work and who they are as a person. To achieve that, I don't shy away from meeting them outside of work just for casual get-togethers during pod outings or team building. I do this because I honestly believe that establishing a trustworthy relationship is a key to success. Remember that keeping relationships professional is vital. You are still the direct manager, and those are your direct reports. After you have the trust of your people, everything is much easier—from making unpopular decisions to giving them constructive feedback. They might not understand it at the very beginning, but they will trust you and will know that you have their side and just want to help them.

As mentioned before, my leadership style has evolved very much. I would say there were three distinctive eras of my leadership style. The first one was when I was extremely friendly and trusting, which led me to being cheated and stolen from. I avoided difficult conversations and giving constructive feedback, which caused me even more trouble. Those were periods when I was stretched the most. In the second era, I became less friendly, sometimes even too tough, and overly controlling. Having bad experiences with trusting too much and having stealing employees led to a situation in which I was involved in everything. At that time, I was a store manager, and I knew everything that happened in the store. I was involved in everything, and no decision could have been made without me. That led to crazy working hours, but somehow, I still managed to score satisfactory results on employee surveys and have a good relationship with most of my employees. With overly controlling managers, relationships with employees deteriorate, and I will address this in the following section. I assume, due to other leadership qualities I showed, my team still followed me. The third phase started not long ago. My current leadership style is a combination of the first two phases: I trust my people, I'm friendly but strict if the situation requires, and I delegate a lot. I don't delegate because I don't want to work myself, but I delegate to develop my people. Trust me, this is sometimes more time-consuming than doing things on my own. However, in order to allow people to grow, it's the only way. I give my direct reports challenging projects and goals, and I support them in fulfilling those. The poetic way to describe my current leadership style would be, "I set the boundaries and give my people free hands to play."

It is important to note that this style does not work with everyone. When we come to the development part, I'll share some amazing examples of exponential growth, but also examples of the people who just cannot cope with this. Then the big question comes: What to do with those people? It's normal that some people do not pursue career growth and are with where they are. If they are good performers, keep to them and make sure they stay happy, motivated, and engaged, as they are your stable bank. They are the ones you can always count on, but more on that later.

The development of my leadership also came with growth on the corporate ladder. I am in a position where working with my people and supporting them takes 70% of my time, if not more. Before, I needed to be much more involved in daily operations and tasks; now, that's on my team, and I'm there to support them. However, the same leadership philosophy can be applied regardless of the level.

DO YOU WANT TO BE A LEADER OR A BOSS?

BOSS

Puts himself first.

Manages the team.

Keeps the responsibility.

LEADER

Puts the team first.

Empowers and inspires the team.

Helps team grow.

Spreads the responsibility.

02
THE POWER

In the following paragraphs, I'd like to discuss the topic of power. In the context of this book, I'm referring to the power a person gets with a position. Anyone climbing up the corporate ladder, regardless of whether the position is managerial or not, will assume certain power. When stepping up to another corporate level, people will look at you differently, and they will take your requests differently. I can tell you the same from personal experience. When I was operations manager and would get requests from an associate director, I would react differently than when I got requests from the same level. That's just human nature.

But what is power? According to the TLEX Institute[iv], the power of human potential is the ability to influence the behavior of others or the course of events. That influence can come from two distinct types of power: positional and personal power. Positional power "is the authority one wields by one's position in an organization's structure and hierarchy." In other words, a manager tells people what they should do, and they do it because their boss told them. You get it with your role, with your title. Next, we have personal power, which is defined "as the ability to influence people and events with or without formal authority. Personal power is more of a person's attitude or state of mind rather than an attempt to maneuver or control others. Its primary aim is self-mastery: competence, vision, positive personal (human) qualities, and service."

Why I'm talking about power in the context of this book? When you become a manager, you get positional power, but if you want to be a leader, you will use your personal power. It is quite easy to give tasks and deadlines to your team and expect those to be fulfilled because you are a boss. Those times are long gone and will not take you far in your career as a people manager. Sure, your team will listen because you are the boss, but engagement and motivation will suffer. People nowadays expect to understand the purpose behind the task, i.e., why they are doing it. You will achieve much greater results if you use personal power to achieve results. It can be quite simple—when giving tasks to your team members, make sure to explain why you are giving a specific task to a specific person. Give them insight into your thoughts and the reasoning behind your decision. Also, explain why this task is important and what benefits its completion will bring. Bring the people on board by explaining the purpose to them, and they will achieve greater results than you expect.

Apart from achieving results better than expected, it can also be an extremely dangerous path if one focuses on positional power only. I worked for a company with a strong hierarchy, and as a part of the senior leadership team, I had no issues with people doing what I asked them. It came with a position, not because they trusted me. In the beginning, I invested a lot of effort in creating an open culture and environment by showing my team I was one of them. I wanted my team to know I was open to hearing their suggestions and opinions about the topics we were discussing, as I didn't expect them to follow blindly every decision I made. I still remember the moment I was discussing a problem with one of the managers in my team. She was a direct report of my direct report, so I was her skip-level manager, which made the situation a bit tougher. She is highly intelligent, knows what she's doing, and is an excellent manager. I started the discussion and asked what she would do to solve issues. The reaction was mind-boggling. She replied: "Oh, I'm allowed to suggest?" You cannot imagine my inner shock. I want my team to challenge me, tell me openly their opinions, and give their own ideas and thoughts about the challenges we were facing. I worked hard to establish myself as a leader that people want to follow. As mentioned, focusing on a positional power only can be a slippery slope for many reasons, but the most obvious here is when you make a stupid decision, your people will not tell you; they will just do it. If we are being honest with ourselves, we all make stupid mistakes from time to time, and I want my team to feel empowered to tell me openly when they think I'm wrong. I want them to do things because they agree with me and believe it's the right thing to do. That comes from using personal power.

Keep in mind that you need to adjust your style of leadership to the situation. There will be moments when you need to cut the discussion and make a final decision. Situations where you will need to jump in and make decisions spot-on without too many explanations will occur. However, that should be an exception. When I was running a store, during busy hours, I didn't always have the luxury to explain the reason behind every decision I made. My team knew that, and they followed because it was not a normal stage. When you have a full store of customers, trucks to unload, and shelves to fill, you need someone who will orchestrate the whole show and give the tasks without a discussion. I still remember my first manager saying, "Sometimes there's too much democracy, and everyone thinks they can have an opinion, but that won't do the job." He is an excellent manager whom I learned a lot from. I adopted a lot of leadership examples from him. He is the leader who gives his team free hands to do their job, but he is there when you need him. When we opened a new store, he called me every morning for two months just to ask how I was doing and if there was something he could do to support me. He didn't do this because he didn't trust me but because he cared. At that time, I was leading a store far away from company headquarters. Once a month, my manager would organize a meeting where all the store managers would meet together. Those were the full day meetings with a lot of important topics on the agenda and decisions that needed to be made. Our manager would let us come to an agreement on a certain topic, and if that was not possible, he would jump in and make a decision. We knew there was nothing we could say after that point, and none of us tried to confront him. We knew we crossed the border, and by continuing discussion among ourselves, we wouldn't achieve anything. We all had 100% trust in him and a deep respect.

The conclusion is you should balance your positional and personal power based on the situation. As with everything in leadership, you need to use common sense and good judgment.

Boss uses

POSITIONAL POWER TO GIVE ORDERS

while Leader uses

PERSONAL POWER TO INSPIRE

03
MICROMANAGEMENT

Let's talk about micromanagement. As per Harvard Business Review[v], micromanagement is "being overly prescriptive on tasks and follow ups — to the point of taking learning opportunities away from your team."

In my personal view, micromanagement is one of the most dangerous phenomena that can hit any organization. You might think this statement is an exaggeration, but trust me, I have seen what consequences one micromanager can have on the organization. In other words, micromanagement is a way of managing your people without giving them freedom. At one point in my career, I exhibited certain traits of a micromanager myself. Although I never told my team how to do their job, I was overly controlling because I felt I needed to own everything myself. There is a terrific book called The Dichotomy of Leadership where, at the beginning, authors are debating how a manager can take too much ownership:

> "Leaders can actually take too much ownership. Yes, with Extreme Ownership you are responsible for everything in your world. But you can't make every decision. You have to empower your team to lead, to take ownership. So you have to give them ownership..."
>
> — *Lief Babin & Jocko Willink*

In my career, I had an opportunity to work with a person who exhibits strong forms of micromanagement. In the beginning, I was not sure what was happening, and I appreciated the curiosity of the person, thinking, *Yeah, that is a newcomer. Of course, the questions are asked.* However, I was very much wrong. Being a manager and leading an organization of more than 80 people, I enjoyed the trust and freedom given by my former manager. He would be there when I needed him, and he set the goals, but reaching those goals and finding the way to do so was strictly on me. All that was changing. As mentioned, I thought that the over-involvement came due to the onboarding phase of my new manager, but I was very, very wrong. My new manager wanted to be informed of everything and know everything that was happening. It's difficult to describe these moments because, by nature, I tend to forget dreadful things. However, I was on the edge more often than not. While this person was genuinely good, he was a complete micromanager. Instead of leading the department strategically and planning for the long term, my manager was involved more in the daily topics than I was. He was frequently reaching directly to my direct reports, giving them tasks, asking for explanations, etc.

That style of leadership dragged me to a point where I completely lost my motivation and engagement. I even stopped discussing with my manager and tried to talk him out of the "brilliant" ideas he came up with. Once, he came to me with an idea to redo a perfectly functioning process. The reason behind this was that he wanted to see what was going on the shop floor. I tried "arms and legs" for days to explain that it just didn't make any sense, and it was not adding any value; it was just creating additional steps. First, even I was not so deep in the process and tracking what was happening in the process to that level, I had my supervisors doing that. Second, asking for something that clearly was a new layer of complexity and not accepting any arguments or feedback— not just mine but other managers related to this topic—is just stupid. After that, I was at a point where if he said a white wall is green, I would agree. Trust me, I'm very vocal about my opinion, and it's hard to change it if I'm not presented with valid arguments. However, I could not do it anymore. I was giving feedback directly to him, but the situation didn't change. In the end, I was lucky enough to be moved to a different manager. The new direct reports of the mentioned manager were experiencing the same scrutiny, which led to some of them leaving the organization. High-potential, talented individuals who loved the company decided to leave as they couldn't cope with that form of harassment. Yes, micromanagement is harassment. If you are not the one micromanaged, but you see this form of behavior in your organization, you should try to stop it, for it can ruin the whole organization.

Give them space. Give them air, I instructed. Let them breathe again. You have to let them make decisions. You have to let them plot the course. You need to tell them the destination, but you need to let them figure out how to get there. You have to let them take ownership—real ownership—of their piece of the mission. Then you will have a team with a culture of true, effective Extreme Ownership and your performance will skyrocket.

— *Lief Babin & Jocko Willink*

04
MY LEADERSHIP RULES

In the coming part, I will share with you leadership rules I strongly believe should be followed by all leaders. The leadership rules I will name are not just mine; they are commonly known and accepted by many, and there are many more.

- Be authentic.
- Lead by example.
- Take responsibility.
- Be decisive.
- Not knowing is ok.
- Avoid blaming.
- Never promise.
- Socialize.
- Always tell the truth.
- Never take credit of your team.

The rules mentioned above are the basics of any leader's behavior regardless of leadership style. Some of them are common sense, yet they are not followed all the time. In the coming section, I'll briefly discuss each of the rules.

BE AUTHENTIC

This is the most important leadership rule. It's quite important, not just in leadership but generally in life. However, we are talking about leadership here. The point of this rule is: Don't fake and don't pretend to be someone you are not. I encountered this term when I got my first job ever. Never before had I actually thought about what "being authentic" means, so this concept was quite new to me. After reading a bit more about it, I thought I understood what lies behind it. However, it wasn't until my first performance review that I fully understood what it meant.

At the beginning of my career, I always thought I had to be louder and more visible because, naturally, I'm not a very outspoken person. I am very strongly opinionated, but I don't have to speak at every given opportunity to be noticed, and I'm not pushy. I used to think I had to be like that to be successful. However, that's not me. I was always the analytic guy who never jumps at the first instance. I need to think everything through, analyze feasible options, and then react. I'm never pushy but considerate. When I had my first performance review, I had a discussion with a Human Resource partner, and I told her I wanted to change that. I had in mind all those loud guys in senior positions who would be owning the meetings. I thought I needed to be like them. She confronted me and said I should never try to change who I am but to enforce it. It is one of the best pieces of advice I was ever given, and that opened my eyes and helped me realize what authenticity means. I was trying to change myself, to change who I am. Being authentic is especially important when you are a manager and a leader. If you want to come to your people as a person they can trust, be who you are.

After reading management books, some people try hard to implement lessons learned. That's valid and a way to go, but don't change yourself. I've noticed a tendency in some who eagerly want to improve and try to implement everything they read, but they lose themselves along the way. The outcome is they appear fake as they just don't act natural anymore. Take the advice to get a better version of yourself, not a different you. I see being authentic as being comfortable with who you are and not trying to cover it up but acting the way you feel—being truthful to yourself and the people around you.

LEAD BY EXAMPLE

This is another rule that should be a pillar of any leadership style. Don't ask from your employees what you don't do yourself. You cannot teach your employees about development if you are not developing yourself. You cannot talk about authenticity and preach it if you're not authentic yourself. Leading by example is being congruent; your words and actions must be in line, and what you say is what you do. A manager should follow the rules set for the whole team; you should never put yourself above the team and act like rules don't apply to you. One of the most common examples is if you don't arrive on time to work, how can you expect your team to do that?

> *"Never forget that your people are watching you. They are looking to you to see what is acceptable behaviour and what isn't. So be the ideal of what you want your people to be."*
>
> *— Robin Sharma*

I'll share with you a basic example of this rule. When I was working in a store, I would always pick up the trash I found while walking around. I also asked my team to do so, but do you think they would be paying attention if they saw me passing by wrappings on the floor? Of course not. I showed them by example what is expected, and soon, all of them were doing so. The store always looked nice and tidy.

Leading by example is one of the tipping points for young managers, from what I have seen so far. Getting a managerial role and a "boss" position can make you think you're above others. Sure, it's not your job to do many tasks, but don't alienate yourself. Leading by example is also showing your team that you're one of them and not just a person who is delegating tasks by helping them when needed and "getting your hands dirty." At the beginning of my career, whenever my team was overwhelmed with work, I would jump in and help them. First of all, I'd make sure all the organizational tasks are taken care of, and then I'll get my hands on something that's "not my job," like replenishing shelves or even working at a cash register, etc. It actually didn't matter what, as long as I was helping. I didn't stop acting like this, but I used the example from the beginning of my career as, at that point, I would really get my hands dirty when I would jump in to help my team.

Jumping in and doing tasks that aren't managerial will show your team that you are there for them when they need you, that they have your support, and that these actions will help you build trust. Keep in mind that it's good to show your team you can also perform some of the tasks because they will think: "If he can do it, I can do it too." Furthermore, you should never ask your team members to do something you wouldn't do yourself.

BE DECISIVE

By being decisive, I'm referring to being able to make a decision and hold up to it. Every leader should have this ability—yet so many don't. Your people will look up to you, and they will expect your guidance, especially if times are tough. While it's ok not to know what to do, sometimes decisions just need to be made, and your job is to make that decision based on available information. I have experienced many times when managers shy away from making decisions and overdo it by requesting additional data just to postpone making the decision for later. This doesn't come up well in front of your team, and it's not a way to go. As said, even if you don't know the right thing to do, sometimes making decisions to the best of your knowledge is what counts, and your team will appreciate it. You will be seen as a capable leader, even if the decision turns wrong. If that happens, hold up to it and learn from it.

Let me pass on a piece of advice. I still remember my dear former colleague and friend, Josipa, who was my coach at the time and whom I was inheriting in my first store. She helped me tremendously when I was just a kid with a degree trying to run the store and be a store manager. I still remember her words when she was leaving—"If there's something you don't know, and you have to make a decision, listen to your heart and do what you think is the best." Now, a lot of people wouldn't agree with that, especially data-driven people. However, here we are talking about leadership, and when people are involved, you cannot always keep a cool head. This piece of advice helped me a lot, and I still use it today when I don't know what to do.

TAKE RESPONSIBILITY

Whatever your team does, it's your responsibility to deal with it. You will be faced with situations that are not your fault, but they are your responsibility to deal with. There's an excellent book by Jack Canfield called The Success Principles. One chapter particularly stands out; it says: "If you want to create the life of your dreams, then you're going to have to take 100% responsibility for your life as well. That means giving up all your excuses, all your victim stores, all the reasons why you can't and why you haven't up until now, and all your blaming of outside circumstances." This is quite powerful, and while it reflects everyday life, it has application in leadership. The author additionally introduces an important equation that goes:

$$Event + Response = Outcome$$

"The basic idea is that every outcome you experience in life, whether it is success or failure, is the result of how you responded to an earlier event or events in your life." When you start behaving with this mindset, your life will be easier. When something goes wrong, it's on you to act, and the way you act will define the outcome. So, the outcome is your responsibility. The same thing goes for when your team does something wrong—it's your job to help them fix it, and you take the blame in front of your boss. Don't throw the team member that made a mistake "under the bus." That's something that no leader should ever do. What if a person is constantly having low performance and keeps making mistakes? Well, it's still your responsibility to deal with it. We'll touch on these points later in the book in more detail.

NOT KNOWING IS OK

At the beginning of my career, I was taught by my more experienced colleagues that I must always know more than my team members, and I should never show any signs of vulnerability and admit I don't know something, as that would ruin my authority. Well, that's completely wrong and quite the opposite of what I experienced later in my career. In the old management mindset, a manager needs to know everything and have all the answers. This is a trap even today some new managers fall into when faced with situations they don't know how to handle or being asked questions they don't know the answer to. First and foremost, it's fine not to know, and it's 100% ok to tell that in front of your team. Some managers think that's a sign of weakness, but it's a sign of self-confidence and strength. Being able to tell your team you don't have the answer or you don't know what to do takes a huge gut to do and makes you a human. Trust me, they will appreciate it more than if you make something up or even lie to them. By doing this, you are also fostering a culture in which it is ok not to know everything, being able to admit it and go from that.

If your team is afraid to admit when they don't know something, how will they learn? If you are a leader, by openly admitting that you don't know everything, you're making it easier for your people to follow your steps and be honest. Only that way can they learn and develop. Also, you, as a manager, cannot know everything, which is why you have your team. They are the experts; they are the ones doing the job, and your duty is to enable them to do so.

"If you don't live an open culture of admitting and adjusting error, your environment won't be either."
— Steffen Reckert

AVOID BLAMING

There will be situations when one of your direct reports will make a mistake, and you will need to jump in to fix the mess. In a situation like that, you can show your team how supportive you are, or you can fail. Based on your behavior, your team will have better or worse opinions about you. So what to do? Primarily, no matter what happens, keep cool and calm. Gather all the facts, get clarity, and see how you can best help to solve the situation. It is irrelevant at that moment whose fault it is, and it's important the situation is handled. Don't lose your temper, and don't blame the person who caused the situation; they are probably feeling bad already, and you won't be helping. After the situation is handled, sit down with the person who caused it and try to understand what the root cause was. Don't blame; everyone can make mistakes as long as they learn from them. Help your employees learn from the situation and understand what they can do not to repeat it.

I've witnessed managers lose their temper and start to yell and blame. That severely deteriorates their image of a good leader and the trust of the team. With behavior like that, they are not fostering a culture where making mistakes and learning is acceptable. Your team will be disengaged, and trust will be low. There was one silly situation, a very risky one, but all went well, luckily. Back in the time when I was store manager, one of my employees was transporting a full pallet of tomatoes weighing around 800 kg. She wasn't careful, made a sharp turn, and the whole pallet of tomatoes fell. Tomatoes were all around the floor. I was passing by. Luckily, nobody got hurt, but my employee was on the verge of crying. I didn't say anything more apart from asking, "Are you ok?" and started collecting the tomatoes and putting them back in the boxes. I could have easily called someone else to help, but I didn't. It took half an hour to finish the work. There was damage, but not a significant one. I didn't say a word to the employee at that time, but I could see that it was very difficult for her to make this mistake. Later in the day, the employee came and thanked me for supporting her and also apologized for the mistake. The most important for me was that she understood how dangerous this was, what could have happened if another person was nearby, and what she could do to prevent it. This was a very silly situation, as I said, but you get the point.

CREATE SAFE ENVIRONMENT

The previous two rules, "avoid blaming" and "not knowing is ok," are leading to creating a safe environment. Being an extremely important topic, I decided to name it as a separate rule. A safe environment means your employees are encouraged to try innovative approaches without fear of being criticized if they fail. It also means your employees can come forward if they make mistakes and get the support they need. I cannot emphasize enough how important it is to foster such a culture so employees can freely learn and grow. Let me give you an example. Back in the time when I was running the store, a new department manager ordered too many fresh products, and those had a shelf life of about a few days. The quantity was about three times what we needed. As mentioned, he was completely new in the company and the role, but he was hard-working and had potential. I remember him coming to my office, completely wet from sweat, barely able to explain what happened with a shivering voice. My first reaction was to tell him to relax, as everyone can make a mistake. The second question was, how can I support him? Since he was very new, I wasn't expecting many suggestions. I immediately informed my sales force team, who got on the field and actively offered the product to our biggest customers at discounted prices as the quantity was just too big. It was better to earn less and sell it than to have so many products with expiring dates. The situation was handled, and I asked my department manager what he learned. Trust me, he never made the same mistake again, but it was also a sign of the culture that we had in the team. There is certainly a limit, and this approach relies on people learning from mistakes. If they continue making the same mistakes repeatedly, you need to react differently, but we'll discuss it in later stages of the book.

The safe environment I'm talking about here belongs to the broader topic of psychological safety at work, which is a topic in itself, so I'm not going to go deeper into the discussion. There is an excellent book on this topic I'd recommend you read called The Fearless Organization, where psychological safety is defined "...as a climate in which people are comfortable expressing and being themselves. When people have psychological safety at work, they feel comfortable sharing concerns and mistakes without fear of embarrassment or retribution. They are confident that they can speak up and won't be humiliated, ignored, or blamed. They know they can ask questions they are unsure about something."

NEVER PROMISE

A big steppingstone for some managers is promising their employees a lot more than they are sure they can deliver. Do not do that. Whether it's a promotion, salary increase, or whatever, never promise it. You should commit to doing your best for a specific outcome, but don't claim it until it's for sure done. There are always situations that you have no influence on, and by promising something that, in the end, won't happen, you'll lose face in front of that employee. Luckily, I have never promised one of my employees something I couldn't do. I would say this is thanks to my mum, who taught me not to make promises I cannot keep. However, I was promised many things by my manager, from salary increases to big projects I'd lead, and most of those promises never came true. You can assume that I lost trust, and I started doubting anything coming from that person, which is less than ideal for a work relationship.

SOCIALIZING

I have a policy that I'm trying to hold up to: I never meet with only one of my direct reports outside of work; it's either that all are invited or no one. I've seen many times in my career managers developing friendship relationships with some of their direct reports, and they were later on not able to make tough decisions when needed. Not only that but also the other team members felt like this particular employee had a better connection to the boss and had additional benefits. Now, whether the latter is true or not, it doesn't matter. What matters in this case is what people think and say. Don't put yourself in this situation because you will have a tough time justifying your actions, especially if it comes to promoting that person.

That also doesn't mean you cannot have friendship with your direct report. When I took over a whole unit in the company I worked for, I was in a position where both of my direct reports were my friends, as we started on the same level at the beginning. However, they both knew I was quite capable of making a distinction between private and professional, and they knew I was not going to make their life easier because of our private relationship. At work, we kept our relationship professional and continued to be friends outside.

ALWAYS TELL THE TRUTH

This should be obvious, and it should be reflected in basic human behavior. The truth always comes out, and your integrity will be ruined. That happened to one of the managers I worked closely with, and his direct reports were openly talking about his tendency to bend the truth, mostly to show himself in a better light. Never lie to your direct reports—they will find out. As a manager, you cannot always disclose everything and ensure 100% transparency, but rather just don't say anything and explain you are not allowed to share more information.

NEVER TAKE CREDIT OF YOUR TEAM

When your team has a great accomplishment, make sure to point that out. Never ever "steal" credits for yourself. You are the manager of that team, and every success is also your success, and there's no need to mention it. Worst case, present it as your own success. I have witnessed this many times, unfortunately. Managers doing that were uncovered very fast, and they also lost the trust of their peers, not just team members.

"Never take credit for people's achievements, but always take some responsibility for their failures."
— ***Stefan Falk***

PART 2:
HIRE

During my career, I have held dozens of interviews and hired dozens of people. I'm not exaggerating. When the new store was opening, I had an interview with almost every employee before they got a yes. I've been a hiring manager many times and many times part of the hiring committee. I learned how important it is to select the right person for the position and how costly it can be if done otherwise. I have to break it to you right at the beginning: I'll not share a magic formula on how to hire the right person as I don't know it myself. It happened so many times I was 100% sure a person would be a high performer and perfect fit, and it was completely the opposite. The truth is you can never know. A person can seem like a perfect fit, have all the right answers, and tick all of the boxes, but they just don't find their way when they start. What I would like to offer in this chapter is advice, steps, and learnings I have from the hiring process to help you minimize the failure rate. If you're not interested in this topic at the moment, feel free to skip to the next chapter.

"I never judge people by their education and qualifications. The first thing we look for at Virgin when hiring new staff is personality, which always wins over book smarts or job-specific skills — the latter can be learned. "

— Richard Branson

01
HIRING FOR ATTITUDE AND POTENTIAL

Every company wants to hire the right people, and I'm sure you want to hire the right people for your team, but what does that actually mean? I've seen too often companies and managers striving to hire top talent based on their skills, education, and work experience. I'm not saying that is something bad at all, but it should not be the only factor and, for sure, not the driving factor. Work experience, education, and skills are certainly particularly important, especially when hiring for a higher position. Personally, those are qualifications I check briefly before the interview, and my focus is on finding out if the person would be fit for my team/company or not. Does the person have the right mindset or the right attitude, and do they fit with the company's culture and company's values? That's what matters the most. I would always rather hire for those traits than for the educational qualifications and skills, for example. Feel free to disagree: I strongly believe that the right mindset beats work-related knowledge—work-related skills are (mostly) easy to learn, but changing someone's mindset is exceedingly difficult. Herb Kelleher, a founder of Southwest Airlines, said, "You don't hire for skills, you hire for attitude. You can always teach skills." I could not agree more.

That is the part that's always tricky to check, as work experience and other hard skills can be easy—attitude, not so much. Big, well-structured companies approach interviews by setting up the panels, and each panel member gets a set of questions they need to ask the candidate. In the company I worked for, the hiring process was organized very well, and to check the cultural fit, each of the panel members (or hiring committee), usually consisting of 4 people, got behavioral questions based on the company's people principles. The point of behavioral questions is to understand how a person acted in a certain situation. By asking a candidate, for example, to tell you about a situation when they had a conflict with a stakeholder and how they resolved it, you get a picture of how that person is collaborating and handling conflicts. After all interviews were conducted, we would meet and discuss the candidate, and a final yes or no was given. With this approach, the company tried to ensure an objective hiring process while making sure the candidate would be the right fit for the company's culture. Small companies or startups usually don't have developed hiring processes like that, but if you're part of such an organization, try to establish such a process to increase your odds of hiring the right person in your team.

Storytime

One of my biggest hiring failures was when I was building the team for the new store. At that time, more than 40 people were hired as core time that would be running the store, and the position in question was Shift Manager reporting directly to me. The person in question already had experience working at a competitor retail chain in a similar position and seemed like a perfect fit. The whole hiring committee had concerns as the company our candidate came from was notorious for focusing on productivity and sometimes pushing people to limits. All of us thought this person would adjust to the people-centric culture my company had at that time. I personally had additional concerns as I was not able to establish any rapport with her during interviews, and she didn't seem authentic at all. However, we proceed with hiring. In the beginning, in the whole craziness of the new store opening, everything seemed to be going in a good direction. After a few months, the issues started arising. First, I realized I couldn't trust her as she was always agreeing with me, and then she changed the narrative behind my back. For me, that's a clear "no-go." If I cannot trust the person who's my second hand, how are we supposed to work together? Secondly, the person was behaving like a proper boss—giving orders and pushing people to the limits—which was completely opposite from the values of the company and the culture I was trying to build in a new store. The situation escalated when she forgot to open the store on time, with customers waiting outside for 30 minutes. She didn't take any responsibility for the failure; she rather blamed everyone else for her own mistake—even me, for giving her too many tasks which she needed to fulfill. While everyone can make mistakes, as we are all human beings, the way you deal with those mistakes shows what kind of person you are. Summing up everything, this person was clearly not for my team, and she was managed out. This is the biggest hiring mistake I made, as I was not reacting to red flags and a cultural mismatch. In all desire to be as objective as possible, soft skills were disregarded, and a person who was a wrong fit was hired.

I also hire for talent or potential. You could argue that both mindset and talent/potential go in the same bucket, but I wanted to make a point here and emphasize it. There are many examples when I rejected people with more experience and better educational backgrounds for someone with the drive to learn and grow. If, during the interview, I see the candidate has the right mindset, has the potential to grow, and has a wish to learn, but they are still not there, I'll give a chance to that person.

Personally, I'm also an example of such a hiring when my first company decided to do just that. I was 26 years old when I became a store manager. The ages of my colleagues in the same position were between 35 and 45, and all of them came to that position working their way up. I finished college and two years of management training program. I had no experience in running a store, let alone running a team. However, they took a risk and made me the youngest store manager in the company ever (to this day, there is no one younger than me). I would say I justified their trust and built my way up. Is this a risky move? Sure, it is, but it's also hiring someone purely based on qualifications. You need to keep in mind that when you hire someone in this way, you will need to invest much more time in training and the development of the person, but it can heavily pay off. Make sure to prepare a good onboarding program.

"Hiring people is an art, not a science and resumes can't tell you whether someones will fit into a company's culture."

— *Howard Schultz*

02
TIPS FOR THE INTERVIEW

How many times did it happen that you had an interview and you felt very bad afterward because the interviewer was a complete idiot? The interview process can improve or deteriorate how a candidate perceives the company. Keep in mind that during the interviews, the candidates are also making assessments of the company to figure out if they want to work at that place. At least that's what I do, and it happened a few times that just based on the feeling I got from the interviewer, I rejected participating in further steps. During the interview, you are the face of the company and have the power to make the entire process nicer for the candidate. That doesn't mean you should not ask challenging questions, but being nice and pleasant goes a mile. The candidates will usually be super nervous, so do your part and make them feel comfortable. Furthermore, be the ambassador for the company. During the interview, I always try to convey the company's culture and explain why the company is a great place to work.

Let me share a few tips. Whether you are a hiring manager or part of the hiring committee, these mentioned apply:

- Understand the position and level you are hiring for: This is to adjust your questions and expectations from the candidate. It's not the same if you're hiring an intern or supervisor.

- Read materials: Go through your CV and highlight the most interesting parts for you and the ones you'd like to check further during the interview.
- Make a list of questions you want to ask: This is vital, as you don't want to make up questions on the spot.
- Be on time: Show respect for the candidate who wants to work at your company.
- Make an ice breaker with small talk (Don't go directly into the interview)
- Make notes and inform the candidate you will be taking those—you don't want the candidate to think you're writing emails
- Be objective.
- Leave the last 10-15 minutes for the candidate to ask questions.

Last piece of advice: Familiarize yourself with the laws of the country you are working in. In some countries in Europe, you are not allowed to ask certain questions, like why a candidate is leaving his current job or if he has some disabilities. Usually, your company will require you to do training before you get to start interviewing, and those will be mentioned there. Just keep in mind that privacy is taken seriously.

You did the interview, so how do you know if the candidate is the right fit for the company and the position? Well, you can never be sure. In my former company, much focus was being put on objectivity during the interview and making decisions solemnly based on facts. That doesn't always work, especially when you have a person in front of you who's telling you all the right words, but the feeling you have is somehow odd. The words don't match the energy. The rule I follow: When in doubt, say no. The last thing you need is to hire a person who might be wrong for the position and the company.

What is important is to keep the standard high. There is a natural tendency to want to lower criteria if it's difficult to find the right person, but you should never compromise on this. There is a substantial risk you will hire a person who is not ready for the position and will struggle a lot to succeed. Or they won't succeed at all but rather fail. So, keep the bar high and leave a position open until you find the right candidate. I had an opportunity to witness wrong hiring—a person was given a level that he was not on and couldn't reach in the future. The person in question was hired as a manager and took over a department in challenging times for the company. He was a fit for the company from a cultural point of view, but he had no previous leadership experience and never led a department. This would not be the issue if he had the potential to grow and develop, but he didn't. To make things worse, that manager was not aware of the tasks and levels they would need to perform. The hiring manager was just looking for someone to fill the position without clearly communicating the expectations and all the challenges the person would face. All that unfortunately resulted in health issues for the person as the pressure and responsibility were just too high for him to cope with. He was set for failure from the very beginning. Need I say, he himself decided to leave. The company lost almost 3 months and a lot of money to bring in and to train this manager, other departments within the company again lost the support, and recruiting for a new person had to begin once again. The point of the story: Don't hire someone just to fill in the position.

03
FAVORITE INTERVIEW QUESTIONS

Now, I'd like to share with you my favorite interview questions that I ask almost every candidate, depending on the position and level I'm interviewing for.

1. **What kind of boss do you like to have, and what are your expectations?**

This question takes candidates by surprise most of the time. Based on this question, I can understand if the candidate has realistic expectations and if I'm able to offer what's expected. It can tell me if a person will be high maintenance, coming with problems and expecting me to solve them, or a self-driven individual seeking support when needed. Also, my saying is that when you are looking for a job, you are not choosing only the position but also the manager. In that sense, candidates should know what kind of person they want to work with.

2. **What do you consider to be your greatest improvement area?**

By asking this question, I seek to understand if a person has developed self-awareness or not. I often get an answer that they want to improve hard skills like knowledge of Excel or project management. In that case, I drill down further to soft skills as I'm also interested in that. The answer I'm looking for is something like:

"I want to improve how I collaborate with difficult peers; I want to work on my coaching skills," etc. These kinds of answers tell me the person takes their personal development very seriously by reflecting and detecting opportunity areas, and they are not ashamed to talk about it.

3. **What would your existing colleagues or team members tell me about you if I asked them?**

This question also has to do with self-awareness but from a distinct perspective. If a person tells me that colleagues or team members would say only positive things about them, it means they are either delusional or a people pleaser, and neither is good. I'm not expecting an exact answer but an assumption that then tells me if a person is thinking about others and the impact their behavior has on their team. The answer could be: "Everyone will tell you I'm the funny one and always cracking the jokes. Not everyone likes my jokes all the time, but I'm working on it." That's telling me about personality but also about self-awareness.

4. **Tell me about a situation when you had to jump in and help your team with the workload they faced. What did you do to help?**

The answer to this question tells me what kind of a manager the candidate is: are they following the old leadership style when they are the boss and that's the team's task, or they don't have issues with rolling up their sleeves and being one of the team when it's necessary? I would ask this question only when hiring for a managerial position, and people I look for need to have a hands-on mindset. Also, I would expect them to tell me they first checked if there are more pressing topics coming their way that urgently need to be taken care of. That shows they learned prioritization and always have a big picture in mind.

5. **Tell me about a time when you introduced a process improvement/general improvement. How did you do it, and what were the results?**

The answer to this question shows me that if a person actually proposed an improvement for their current job, are they proactive and thinking about what can be done better or more efficiently? It can be that they were just told to do so. Furthermore, if a candidate did it in a structured and organized way and is able to describe it, it tells a lot about how they approach work in general. The last piece, what were the results, shows if they actually thought about the impact and if they measured it. This can show a bit about the analytical competencies a candidate has.

6. **Can you remember the last time you had to take a calculated risk / make a difficult business decision? How did you approach this?**

The reason I ask this question is to understand the thought process of a candidate, whether they reacted impulsively or they actually thought it through. Did they make a data-driven decision, or was it based on gut feeling? It shows a balance between being analytical and trusting experience and judgment of the situations. I cannot give examples of the answers I expect. Sometimes, it's needed to make a snap decision, and you don't have time to go through a bunch of data, so you need to work with what you have. In that sense, the expected answer really depends on the situation the candidate explains.

7. Where do you see yourself in 5 to 10 years?

This is the essential question for understanding what the candidate plans for the future and wishes for development are. I ask this question among the last ones, as by then, I already get a good picture of the candidate's potential and estimation of how high a candidate could go on a corporate ladder. Some candidates are eager to grow and develop, and others will be content by staying on the current level. Depending on the situation and role you are hiring for, you might be looking for someone who wants to grow within the company and who has the potential to develop at least two positions higher than the one they are being interviewed for. On the contrary, you might be hiring for a role where there is no further potential for development, and you need someone to do a good job on the current level. This question is a check for alignment between candidate wishes and company needs.

Those are the questions candidates will most likely get. The set of questions depends on the role I'm interviewing for. If the role is a leadership one, I'll ask more behavioral questions from the area of leadership and team management. For example, I could ask them to tell me about a situation when they had to manage a team or a tricky situation within the team to understand the skills the person has with managing direct reports and estimate leadership potential. Conversely, if the position is an individual contributor, like a project manager, I'll focus my questions on deliverables and projects the person worked on. I'd ask the candidate to explain to me the situation when they had a tight deadline to deliver a project and what steps they took. This helps with understanding how the person is handling the stress of meeting deadlines and prioritizing. Since most individual contributor positions also require collaboration with people the person doesn't have any authority over, I ask questions about stakeholder management. An example of the question can be to explain a situation when the candidate persuaded a stakeholder to view the situation differently in order to achieve a common goal.

I will also adjust questions to the level of position. Different sets of questions will be asked of a candidate for an internship or entry-level position compared to more senior levels. For internship and entry-level candidates, I'd focus on understanding the potential for future development and the motivation behind applying for the company. Sometimes, people who are just starting their career can have difficulties with knowing what it is that they want and what is the direction they want to go. Or they know it, but they face difficulties formulating it. That's why the set of questions I ask is intended to understand what the candidate actually wants, if they are fit for the company culture, and if they are willing to develop in the company.

Please have in mind one thing. I've stated many times what my expected answer to the question I asked. In case I get an answer contrary to my expectations, I'm not going to cross off the candidate immediately. It depends on the overall picture and all the answers combined. For example, if, based on the answers, I conclude the candidate is having trouble with giving feedback, but still, based on all others, they are fit for the position, I recommend them to note that the opportunity area is handling difficult conversations.

To support you with interviews, you can find additional resources at leadernotaboss.org

PART 3:
DEVELOP

The goal of every manager should be to make himself replaceable; in other words, to train and develop his direct reports so that they are able to perform independently and later on their level. When a team can work without interference from a manager, that manager has done a great job. There are some who fear for their positions and hence don't delegate and don't invest enough time in developing their team. That approach is just outdated. I was always working on making myself not needed because that meant that I could go to another position or take on additional responsibilities. That should be the goal of every manager.

> *"Give a man a fish and you feed him for a day. Teach him how to fish and you feed him for a lifetime."*
>
> — *Chinese proverb*

01
YOUR TEAM MEMBERS

Before discussing the topic of development, it's important to categorize different team members you will face, as they need to be approached in slightly different ways. When talking about development and coaching, I distinguish high performers, stable banks, and low performers.

- **High performers** are your top talents who regularly exceed expectations and often perform on a level higher than theirs; they want to grow and develop and have the potential to do so.
- **Stable banks** are good performers, delivering on expectations; they are willing to learn and develop but on their own level. They don't have big career aspirations.
- **Low performers** are performing below expectations. They could have a wish to grow and develop but are not delivering.

Let's discuss how to approach each of those groups and what strategies and tools you can use.

HIGH PERFORMERS

You will, hopefully, have those on your team, and you need to approach them in the right way. Those are the people who won't be held by throwing money at them. I'll talk about this more in the next chapter. They want continuous challenge, growth, and a steep learning curve. What I do with direct reports like that? I give them tasks that are stretching them to the next level. I try to involve them in the project that I'm leading, and I would normally do all the job myself. However, if I see there's a development opportunity for one of my team members, I'll gladly involve that person. I'll give them my full support at the beginning, and then they'll be performing on their own. Keep in mind that such an approach takes a lot of your time, and you are delegating tasks you would normally do in 50% of the time you have to invest now. But guess what? It's your job to develop people. As mentioned earlier, the more you climb on the corporate ladder, the higher percentage of your time goes into delivering through your team, not as an individual contributor.

Storytime

There are many examples of my direct reports I could share, but there's one case I'm very proud of. Marco was one of the associates in my organization who grew to team lead and later to a manager position. I didn't contribute much to his growth from associate to team lead position, but I have noticed him. Once he became a team lead, we started working closer together, and I started seeing his potential even more. Marco is very smart, extremely curious, likes to take on new challenges and learn, and has a super positive attitude, which, in general, I appreciate in people. In order to support his development, I involved him in projects and delegated to him tasks that even he was sometimes unsure he'd be able to deliver. With each task he successfully completed, he got better and better. He got exposure and visibility that a team lead rarely gets. At the time, we were completely redoing one part of the process, and we needed to create new processing stations. I connected him to the stakeholders and let him lead the discussion on what was needed. He was the expert in this process and knew what his team needed to be able to perform even better. After conducting thorough research, Marco gathered feedback and was actively proposing changes to the variations of the design. I was just a support and a person that was pushing when required. Since the project was high level with a lot of interest from directors, we had to get an official sign-off. There was a meeting with around 10 people, all senior managers and directors; usually, that would be a meeting that my manager would be leading, but he was using the same method as me and let me lead high-profile projects. The new design of processing stations would be discussed, and I invited Marco to present it as he was the one leading the design phase, and it was his time to shine. Need I say that he absolutely rocked it? It was amazing to see how well and articulated he answered all the questions from big shoots. After the meeting, I remember seeing him; he was shaking. I asked what was wrong, and the answer was completely unexpected. He replied something along the lines of, "I started in the company as an associate six months ago, and now I'm participating in meetings with directors. I could never imagine that." And that was true. From that project, everyone knew Marco was a superstar. Within six months in the team lead role, he applied for a managerial position and completely nailed the panels, which resulted in him getting a second promotion within half a year. To get one thing straight, he was a talented and high performer before me. Maybe he would perform even better with some other manager, but he would for sure not have such exponential growth without a manager recognizing his potential, giving him challenges, and supporting him along the way. However, it takes more to manage people like that and help them grow. I still say he's responsible for his fast development. I gave him opportunities and opened the doors for him, but he was the one taking everything offered and doing the hard job.

STABLE BANKS

I mentioned that not everyone will want to have huge career growth and make an additional effort. That is perfectly fine. If those people are good performers and are still willing to learn and improve themselves within their current roles, those are your stable banks, and you should hold on to them. Invest time in them; don't disregard them. You need to keep them motivated and engaged, the same as your high performers. The process will be similar to the other group: understand what their expectations and goals are and what you can do to support them. The fact that those people are stable banks and don't want to climb the corporate ladder doesn't mean they don't want to develop and grow. The people I worked with, whom I have identified as stable banks in my teams, still wanted to develop and learn, just on the same level. While you'll challenge high performers with tasks and responsibilities from a level above, you'll challenge stable banks with new responsibilities from their current level.

Storytime

I had one direct report, a manager, who was happy where he was and had no interest in developing to the next level. He did have the potential to do it, but he was happy with his current situation and wanted to have a stable work-life balance where he could spend more time with his family. I 100% respected that. However, he had big ideas on what he wanted to achieve with his department, and I supported him. He had a vision of how to improve processes and provide a better experience for our customers. Later on, he wanted to get a new challenge on the same level, so I changed his departments, and he was again learning and growing. I was very content with his performance as he was a person I could always count on. Take care of these people; they are an integral part of your team.

LOW PERFORMERS

Low performers are the individuals who are performing and delivering below the expectations of their current role and level. My approach to dealing with low performers is to first check if they understood the expectations. Afterward, I clearly communicate to the person they are not meeting those mentioned expectations. More on critical feedback in the following chapters. The following step is to understand the whole situation and to get their side of the story: why they think this is the case and what is contributing to it. The last is understanding how I can support them in achieving better performance and agreeing on an action plan to get there.

There are various reasons people have low performance, and most of the time, it is not because they are lazy and don't want to work. That's why understanding the situation is crucial. It can happen your team member is lacking the skills that will enable him to perform on the required level. Identifying those and supporting your team member with a concrete training plan is an easy solution. Another possibility is that your employee has a tough time in their private life, which is then reflected in work life. While we should not allow our performance at work to suffer due to personal issues, in reality, we are all humans, and sometimes, it is impossible to detach. Seek to find the best way to support your team member; maybe that's additional time off or reduced workload during some period of time. After a deeper view of the situation, it can happen the person is just not for the role. If that's the case, support your employee to find the role that's the right fit for them.

Storytime

To give a bit of background, I had inherited the manager, who was really an expert in what he was doing. Let's call him Lucas. Lucas had elaborate technical knowledge of the machines and tools we used, and he was trustworthy. However, he had no leadership skills, and, at that time, he was leading one of the biggest teams in my organization. His promotion happened way before I came to the company and was obviously without the company's people principles in mind. Lucas was not working with his team at all; rather, he spent time behind the computer and fixing machines. That resulted in very low engagement, which led to low productivity. At that point, I already had conversations with him about low productivity, and I heard only excuses and how nothing could be done apart from adding more people—which doesn't increase productivity, obviously. In every discussion we had, he didn't provide any solution or intent to try something new to improve the situation. He was just bringing the problems. The issue became even more obvious when the leadership counterpart shift was taken over by new managers who implemented many changes and seriously increased engagement and productivity. Instead of asking colleagues what they did better and what he could improve, Lucas kicked off his investigation and claimed the other team was faking numbers, which wasn't true. Something needed to be done. That was the moment when I did the performance grading based on company principles, and I couldn't have been more surprised when one of the lowest performers graded his overall performance above expectations. Since this was quite early in the performance cycle, I was able to explain all his opportunity areas. However, this was a very, very difficult conversation. I knew in advance a particular individual had high opinions about his performance, in spite of them not being suitable for this role at all. Knowing how hard it could be, I prepared myself thoroughly. We discussed what might be the problem, and he agreed his leadership skills were not good. Furthermore, we agreed he was in the wrong position as he should be taking an expert path, not a people manager path, for his career development. We agreed to follow up the following week about what his proposal for a way forward would be. It was actually a good discussion, and I thought we were going somewhere. In the meantime, I already had alignment with the leadership team and with the human resources, and the decision was unanimous: Lucas could not stay in this role. In our new meeting, Lucas said he would look for opportunities outside of the company since there was no role within the company that would require his skill set. I was more than happy with this development. I gave him time to look for other roles. However, nothing was happening, and he wasn't getting the sense of urgency. In the meantime, his behavior became very toxic, and he started causing real issues among other teams. I couldn't keep him anymore and decided he needed to leave with an immediate effect.

This story is one of the more difficult cases I had to deal with. Depending on the situation, you can take different strategies. If your team member is open and willing to improve, with your support and clear actions, they can become a stable performer. In the worst case, if there are no reasons for low performance and the person is not showing the will to improve, you should proceed with an official performance improvement plan (explained at the end of this chapter). In the story I told you, I couldn't use a performance improvement plan as Lucas was in a completely wrong role.

Those were the three types of team members I identified when it comes to performance and development potential. In the following chapters, I'll discuss tools you can use to support your team members and help their development.

02
ONE-ON-ONE'S

The question is how to approach the development of your direct reports. You need to get to know your people. Not just who they are at work but also who they are outside of work. This is crucial for establishing a trustful relationship. You need to understand where they want to develop further and what their goals are. This is usually done in regular weekly meetings called one-on-one (1:1). I would dare to say the name is self-explanatory. Those meetings are an opportunity to interact with your team members, to listen to them, and to understand their points of view. It should be a platform to improve working relationships and help your employees with issues they might be facing. A weekly cadence would be my suggestion. You can meet more than once a week, if necessary. This proposal works when you have a team of up to 10 direct reports. If you're working for a company where it's common to have more than 10 direct reports, consider shifting to a bi-weekly basis. There are a few rules of 1:1 you should keep in mind:

IT'S A MEETING FOR YOUR DIRECT REPORT, NOT YOU

Managers sometimes tend to "steal" the meeting and discuss topics that are relevant to them. You should never do that. Make that time about the employees you're meeting with. You should have your points, but let the direct report lead the meeting and follow his agenda.

1:1 IS NOT A BUSINESS UPDATE

Don't confuse the 1:1 with business updates; it's a development meeting, and everything should revolve around that. You can discuss projects and progress updates if your employee needs support, but don't come with the expectation that you will discuss KPIs and bridge the targets. That's not the point of 1:1.

NEVER MISS 1:1

In the world of craziness where deadlines need to be met, it's easy to get into the temptation to skip regular 1:1—but you should never do that. First of all, your main task as a people manager is to "manage" or, better say, lead your people. Weekly meetings are a perfect opportunity for that. This is an opportunity for your direct report to ask you questions, raise concerns, and seek your support. Basically, it is an opportunity for them to speak what's on their mind. You should never take that away from them. Sometimes, it's difficult, but having had regular 1:1 with 8 direct reports for a few months, you can do it.

As said before, one-on-ones are for your employees, and you should follow their agenda, but also come with points. 1:1 being a development meeting, you should regularly discuss the performance of your employees. That discussion should revolve around goals that you set with your direct report that they have to achieve in a given timeline. Whenever there is a concern, you should address it. This is very important, as you don't want your employees to think they are doing great when the reality is different. If your company has a performance review, when the time comes, you want to be already aligned with your employees on their performance so as not to have any uncomfortable surprises. That's why you should always share constructive feedback and discuss the performance of your direct report.

Furthermore, use those meetings and get feedback from your team members. Like any relationship, a work relationship is two-way street; it works in both directions. Your employees will probably be confused at first, but give them the opportunity to share direct feedback about you directly with you. The information you get can help you grow as a leader and also strengthen the relationship with your team members.

> *"Get constant feedback about your leadership style and the things that you are doing to make sure you are still on the right path."*
>
> — *Steffen Reckert*

03
FEEDBACK

Difficult conversations or constructive feedback is an essential part of any people leader's daily work. Sometimes, those are minor things, but sometimes, you need to discuss serious topics with your direct reports. At the beginning of my career, I had issues having constructive conversations with my team members. I would postpone it for days and have a stomachache when the time came, and I couldn't postpone it anymore. Over time, it became easier, and I learned the hard way I needed to immediately raise my concerns. Now, my team knows they can always expect straightforward feedback from me during our one-on-ones, whether they like it or not. Most of them do, as they know everything I tell them is for their own good. One of my best-performing team members, who is an extremely talented young leader, is so used to getting a lot of feedback from me. It became that if a situation about which I wanted to pass my feedback happened while we were together, he already knew what I'd tell him even before I said a word. He'd then take it and take visible actions. That's a joy to experience. In this chapter, I'll share with you situations from which I learned a lot about difficult conversations and tips on how to execute those and make them easier.

Storytime

There is, however, one situation that I'm not proud of at all, but it taught me a lot. I failed to have a direct confrontation, and it completely shattered that relationship. The story goes back a few years. I was a store manager at that time and was getting ready to move to a brand-new store much bigger than mine at that time. The person who was supposed to replace me was one of my colleagues from the same management trainee program our company had. We were both quite young at that point. I was 27, and he, let's call him Thomas, was one year younger than me. Thomas was about to spend 6 months in my store, learning from me, before officially taking over the whole store. Thomas, while a genuinely good person, was very much concerned by social status to the point where he would already present himself as a manager while he was still in training. We had quite a fun time outside of work, but at work, things were not going in the right direction. Thomas was exhibiting the behavior of old-fashioned managers where he was a big boss, and others needed to do what he told them. I raised my concerns to our manager, and he took it. The situation didn't change, and it just got worse. My team, used to my leadership style with a hands-on approach, didn't appreciate that behavior. There were many complaints coming to me about the new manager's behavior. The thing was, I was still the official manager, and that was still my team. I didn't want to leave them in the hands of a person who clearly didn't have leadership capacity. I escalated the situation once again to our manager, who involved HR, and Thomas was immediately removed from the store. While I strongly believe that's the best outcome, the way I handled the situation is not something I'm proud of. Even though I did all of the steps to leave my team and store in good hands, I failed to have an open conversation with Thomas before raising issues to our boss. I was giving him hints in the hope that he would learn from my example, but that was not enough. Indeed, he was not reporting to me, but I was supposed to support his development, which I didn't. I avoided difficult conversations and confrontations with him. Would the situation have developed in a different way if I had that feedback talk? I doubt it. Based on the feedback I gave to our manager, he had strong conversations with Thomas, and nothing changed. There are certain personality traits that cannot be changed, and Thomas was just not leadership material for that company. Maybe in other companies, he would strive, but I see him more as an individual contributor. However, our relationship was completely shattered when he got removed from a position, and I know I should have done more. I should have told him everything directly and then extended my concerns to our manager—one important lesson I'll always carry with me.

Contrary to all other stories in the book, this one describes a peer-to-peer relationship. In business, we don't face only difficult situations with our team members; sometimes, it's also necessary to give direct feedback to our peers, no matter how hard it is. Coming back to managing team members, over time, I learned that you need to be very clear when sharing feedback with your employees. Your team members need to understand and accept what you are sharing with them. Let me explain.

Storytime

I had a direct report who was not meeting the bar of his level. This employee, let's call him Nico, had a lot of knowledge and used to be a solid performer. However, the former manager was more of a friend to Nico than a manager and was giving him better grades than he deserved, which contributed to Nico expecting a good grade on the performance review again. We had regular discussions, and I was always giving him open and honest feedback. Nico was always understanding my feedback, and he was even agreeing with it. However, I failed to express clearly what grade he would get in the performance review if the situation didn't change. The company I was working for at that time had a biannual performance review, and all of us were graded against people's principles. To ensure direct reports are going in the right direction, it was important to provide them with grading a couple of times during performance cycles. I didn't do that as it was not officially required by the company, but I learned the hard way to always do it. When the review came, it was obvious Nico was "sometimes below our high expectations," which is the exact term the company was using to explain grade 4 on a 1 to 5 scale (1 being the best, 5 the worst). In that company, we had pre-calibration meetings where we would discuss all employees on the same level. All of my colleagues confirmed the grade given to Nico. Following the review closure, I was able to communicate individual results to my team members in one-on-one sessions. The meeting with Nico didn't go well at all. While I was giving feedback and emphasizing opportunity areas, he agreed with everything I said. However, once I mentioned the actual grading, he completely disagreed. We had a rather heated discussion, and it took a few weeks for Nico to take the feedback and accept it. You could say it's strange the employee agreed with the outlined opportunity areas but completely disagreed with the grade. Here, I realized that I have failed by not giving straightforward performance reviews more often towards the official performance cycle. So, I strongly encourage you to make this a habit and align with your direct reports on how they are performing toward their goals. From this example, I also learned that even though people might be receptive to feedback, to make a strong case, explain the consequences they might face if they don't improve.

The mentioned example has a twist. As my former manager would say, the performance review rating was a "hit the wall moment" for this employee. After a few weeks, Nico took the feedback and seriously started working on his opportunity areas. He became more proactive, he took initiatives himself without waiting for direct tasks, and he tremendously improved his communication and presentation skills. Within a few months, his efforts started to be noticed by my colleagues and the whole leadership team. By the next review, the employee already got a "meeting our high expectation" grade. It was indeed a remarkable comeback, and I believe our relationship had something to do with it. Like with all my direct reports, I try to establish a trust-based relationship. In this case, the employee realized I had his best interests in mind and cared about him getting to higher levels of performance. Hence, it is not proven, but in my opinion, he digested the review outcome easier and took the feedback seriously.

The point of the story is that no matter how difficult, don't avoid sharing constructive feedback with your direct reports. For sure, it's not going to be easy for them to hear and for you to tell, but postponing will not do any good. As soon as you notice something, prepare yourself thoroughly and convey the feedback.

GRADE EMPLOYEES BASED ON COMPANY STANDARDS

If your company has leadership guidelines, people principles, or any other publicly available set of values against which every employee is graded. Using your company principles, you're not comparing your employees against each other but against the bar that has been set.

PREPARE ACTUAL EXAMPLES AND FACTS

Have real situations and examples when your employee failed to perform on standards. Avoid using your feelings when giving feedback in a way *"I feel this...."* Make sure to prepare facts on which your feedback is based.

CALIBRATE WITH YOUR COLLEAGUES ON THE SAME LEVEL/MANAGER/HR

If you are unsure whether your judgment is right, discuss your individual with a peer who is able to make an objective comment based on work experience. Inform your direct manager and HR if you believe the case will be difficult to handle and get their opinion as well.

PLAN THE CONVERSATION

Although it might sound silly, take time to plan a conversation: how the conversation might go, what you will say, and when. Giving constructive feedback is not easy, especially if you are a new manager. My advice is to always prepare yourself; it will help you guide the conversation and make it a bit easier.

BE EMPHATIC

The point of difficult conversations is to help your team member work on their opportunity areas, which will enable them to grow and not bring someone down. You should approach the conversation with full empathy and understanding and ensure your employee knows you have their best interests in mind.

GIVE STRAIGHTFORWARD FEEDBACK

I've never been a fan of so-called sandwich feedback. The method calls for cushioning negative feedback with positive; you should first deliver positive, then negative, and finish with positive feedback. It's also known as the "Shit Sandwich" among opponents of the method as it can be very confusing and give mixed understanding. My advice is to give straightforward feedback without a place for interpretation. You should acknowledge all the positive aspects and provide appreciative feedback. Then, make sure opportunity areas (or critical feedback) are clearly emphasized and that your employee understands them. Don't try to make it nicer, as your employee could miss the point.

GIVE TIME

Receiving constructive feedback from a manager is not always easy, and some team members might be completely taken aback. Acknowledge that they might need time to process the feedback. With that in mind, offer an additional appointment where you can discuss the feedback after it's settled.

03
COACHING

"Before you are a leader, success is all about growing yourself. When you become a leader, success is all about growing others."

— *Jack Welch*

Coaching is one of the vital tools managers have at their disposal to use for the development of direct reports. Yet, it's oftentimes very much disregarded. What is coaching about? Coaching is a non-directive form of development focusing on improving performance and developing an individual.[vi] Fundamentals of coaching is about asking the right questions and providing enough space so that your employees can reach their goals and improve their skills themselves.

You might be wondering, how is that relevant for you? Your team members will come to you with all kinds of questions and problems, and it's your task to support them in solving them. The way you do it will define their growth. If your employee comes to you and asks what they should do in a specific situation, and you give them the answer, they'll just continue coming to you whenever they have any questions. Your team member won't think with their own head; rather, they'll rely on you to solve every issue that comes their way. That's not how you develop an employee, as they won't be growing.

Instead, start asking them questions: What are the options? Which option would they choose? In that way, your team will start thinking for themselves and start solving problems without you. I know it's much easier to just answer the question instead of spending some time guiding your employees in the right direction, so they come to the conclusion themselves. However, as people leaders, our main job is to grow our team; hence, coaching is essential.

With my first team, I had a tendency to jump in whenever there was some sort of situation and wanted to answer all of the questions. That made them dependent on me, and I was not supporting their development. Also, as business was evolving, I had more and more on my plate, and I just couldn't answer all the questions, solve all the problems, and be there all the time. I needed to change my strategy and empower my team to start making decisions on their own, which was challenging as they were used to me solving everything. I started asking questions to guide them in the right direction and allowed them to make the conclusion. Slowly, I raised the bar and expected my team, when talking about the problem, to offer a proposal of what they would do in a specific situation. After a while, they stopped aligning with me on basic questions and started executing on their own. There will be situations that are above their level, and your involvement will be highly needed, but still ask them for even partial solutions. It was time-consuming, but in the end, it paid off. Remember the first chapter: you want your team to work without you, and coaching is part of their development in that direction. Don't be a problem solver for your team.

One important note: Coaching is not the same as mentoring. Mentoring is directive. It's about sharing knowledge and giving advice. To your direct reports, you are a coach, but to your skip levels, you can be a mentor. Mentors are experienced and influential people who can provide guidance. They are usually people who are a few levels above mentees.[vii] When I first started as a management trainee, I was part of a very well-structured program that required me to have a coach and a mentor. The coach was always my direct manager, while mentors were exclusively C-level. My first mentor was the chief finance officer, followed by CEO of the company.

04
INDIVIDUAL DEVELOPMENT PLAN

In previous paragraphs, I discussed how to develop your team in a broad way. Now, it's time to be more tactical. Before starting, it's important to understand that the development of your team members is not performance management. Development means supporting your high potentials to grow to another level and helping your stable banks increase their knowledge and develop horizontally. Performance management and how to deal with low performers will be discussed in the next chapter. The following part will be a discussion about goal setting and individual development plans. As said before, when you have a team, you are expected to deliver through them, meaning the majority of your time will be spent managing, better yet leading, your team. A big chunk of that time you lead them should be focused on their development. So, how do you do it?

1. UNDERSTAND THE AMBITION

My approach always includes understanding the development aspirations of each of my team members. Here, I'm not going to make any distinction between high potentials and stable banks; the approach can be the same. I usually ask my team members where they see themselves a year, 3 years, and 10 years from now. Having these different timelines helps me understand how fast they want to develop and in which direction they want to go. I'm very much aware I cannot support my team member in their 10-year goal, but it helps to put things into perspective. Personally, when I had this discussion with my manager, in 3 years, I see myself in the corporate world and climbing up the corporate ladder, not necessarily in operations and logistics. However, I cannot say the same for my 10-year plan, and that makes the difference. Coming back to my team. Here, the challenge can be if a person isn't self-aware enough and has goals they will find very difficult to achieve. Now, yes, nothing is impossible, but let's be real: no matter how hard I want to be the best football player in the world, it's kind of difficult to get there as I can hardly hit the ball. So, let's just be honest and agree that not all goals are achievable. Have a constructive conversation and give direct feedback to your employees on what you think is possible and what is not.

2. JOINTLY DEFINE THE GOALS

After understanding the ambition, I then start a discussion around 1-year and 3-year goals. I usually spend time discussing how far my direct report is from this goal. The challenge here can be if a person has an unrealistic timeline for achieving the goal. Even though the potential is there, if a team lead I discussed earlier told me he wants to become a senior manager a year from that moment, we would have a constructive conversation. After you are aligned on the 1-year and 3-year goals, you can define them and write them down. Needless to say, the goals should be SMART (specific, measurable, attainable, relevant, and time-bound). Once it's written, it requires a commitment from both sides —your employee working towards it and you to support them.

3. GOALS

The next is defining what steps are necessary to be taken to achieve this goal and over what period of time. Discuss what the path to achieving the goal might look like. Openly discuss opportunity areas your employees need to work on that will enable them to achieve this goal. I encourage my team members that, based on opportunity areas, they should propose actions that they think will help them develop and overcome that particular gap. Those actions can be in the form of training, online courses, or actual live training spanning over a few days. One of my team members, who wanted to improve his analytical skills and data processing knowledge, took from basic to advanced Excel courses on Coursera. The other one needed to open his horizons about leadership, so I assigned him a book to read. When I was doing my first IDP with my managers, they even participated in certain meetings and were put in situations where they could learn more. The opportunities are endless.

Storytime

One of the managers from my organization, let's call him David, wanted to go to the next level. David was not believing in himself, but after repeated conversations with him, David was sure he could do it. David was a great manager. He cared for his team, and at the same time, he was tough and asked for performance. He was always on top of everything and delivered great results. If I needed something to be done, I could always go to him, and the task would be sorted out in no time. While I never had any issues, my peers and other managers from David's level would complain about him as he had difficulties with collaborating and accepting rejection from other teams. He was laser-focused on what must be done within our team, and he did not have a big picture or try to understand why other teams could not support us sometimes. David needed to overcome this in order to go to the next level. I wanted to support as much as I could.

We had a few sessions of discussion about his opportunity areas, and we both aligned on what he needed to work on to develop himself in this role. Being completely open and having his interests in the first place, I suggested he take a position outside of my team. There was an open role on the same level, but that required exquisite collaboration skills. In addition, it involved collaborating with all teams from our business unit and beyond with corporate. In my mind, it was a perfect challenge. David would need to develop the skills he was missing for him to grow to another position. Also, by performing in this role, he would be able to show himself in a new light and build much-needed visibility. With this step, it meant I was losing one of the top-performing managers from my team, but that didn't matter in this situation. My goal was to support David in getting to the next level.

When you are working on action points with your employees that will bring them forward, be completely open because it might not be the most obvious way. Make sure that you define action points that will be in the best interest of your employee, even if that means you "lose" a valuable team member. You should never hinder someone's development because you cannot lose that person. It's your job to develop that person, and it's not their fault you haven't built a succession bench; it's yours. Tough life.

4. CREATE AN INDIVIDUAL DEVELOPMENT PLAN

After actions are defined, put concrete dates by when actions need to be achieved. Keep in mind that dates need to be realistic. Furthermore, don't be shy to involve additional departments, like Human Resources or the Learning/Training team (depending on how your company is structured), in helping with the plan. In case the courses are needed, those folks should be able to help you. Now, remember the process of creating an individual development plan will take a few weeks for sure, and that's normal. Allow yourself enough time to make sure all the inputs are valid, and that the development plan will actually be helpful to your employee, not just another exercise. To help you out with individual development plans, you can find a template at leadernotaboss.com. I adopted this structured approach to development from my first manager. It really helps when you have written actions and stick to them.

5. MONITOR THE PROGRESS

Once the plan is agreed on, make sure to have regular monthly catch-ups. I usually use one of the weekly 1:1s to discuss progress on the plan. Together with my team members, we discuss the actions from the plan they executed, what the challenges were, and what the learning was. Sometimes, there's a tendency to quickly go over the actions without discussing learnings, but if my team member invested time in doing some training, I want to know what they learned. Then, we discuss what actions are coming and if my support is needed.

NOTE!

Make sure your employee understands their development lies in their hands and that it's their responsibility. Your responsibility is to enable them to develop and support them along the way, but that's all you can do. Also, when you create an IDP, be clear to your employees that if a plan includes a goal that they are ready for the next role in 1 year, that doesn't mean they will get it. You will support them and their ambition, but knowing what will happen in one year and if there will be a possibility for you to promote your employees is tough. As mentioned before, don't make promises like this.

Template for IDP can be found at leadernotaboss.org.

05
PERFORMANCE IMPROVEMENT PLAN

A performance improvement plan (PIP) is used to manage (improve) the performance of low-performing employees, and that's what makes it different from an individual development plan (IDP), whose goal is to develop your high-performing employees and stable banks. With that being said, PIP is usually the last resort; it's used when open conversations, feedback, and performance reviews are not providing the desired progress in the performance of an employee. To emphasize the gravity of PIP - it has a limited duration of about 6 months, and if after that period, there is no progress and the employee shows no improvement, it usually results in the termination of the work contract. So PIP, indeed, is a big thing.

Since the performance improvement plan is formal, when you want to "put your employee on PIP," they are not going to be happy at all. My advice is that prior to putting someone on PIP, you align with your manager, and since PIP can have tough consequences, the involvement of Human Resources is a must from the very beginning. Before communicating to your employees that you are putting them on PIP, prepare yourself for any difficult conversation, as it's not going to be easy.

What does the PIP look like? Similar to IDP, in PIP, a concrete action plan with measurable goals should be outlined, but this time, the goals are aligned with the level of position the person is holding. Goals should be SMART, like with IDP. Contrary to IDP, where you and your team members are setting the goals and creating the plan together, PIP is created by you, and it's aligned with business targets. As mentioned, duration over a period of 6 months is common for such a plan. You want to make sure to have regular monthly updates on the progress of PIP with your employee in the presence of HR. Since PIP can have unwanted consequences if your employee shows no sign of progress, use these meetings to be as candid as possible about their performance. You want to avoid a possible misunderstanding and be clear about whether your employee's performance is satisfying or not.

Keep in mind that a performance improvement plan is not a tool to get rid of someone; it's used to help low performers. Over time, I've seen managers putting employees they want to release on PIP and setting unattainable goals. This case should be avoided as you are just wasting everyone's time, and there are other ways to do that. To help you out, you can find a template for PIP at leadernotaboss.org.

06
ADDITIONAL TIPS DEVELOPMENT

Here are a few general tips to keep in mind when it comes to people development, regardless of which tool you are using.

CHALLENGE, BUT DON'T BURN YOUR PEOPLE

The advice I gave on developing your high performers is based on stretching and challenging them to grow to the next level. As mentioned earlier, I usually give those people projects or tasks above their level to create opportunities for their growth, as I believe growth happens outside of the comfort zone. However, be mindful. When you have direct reports that are still unsure, you have to be very careful with them and guide them along the way. In the beginning, you need to be close to their side and reassure them. Make sure they know you trust them and you are sure they can do it. There's also a question every manager in this position should ask themselves: Is the challenge big enough, or is it too much? In my career, I had two managers I looked up to who helped me grow and develop into the leader I am today. One of them was always saying, "Challenge drives innovation." He's the person that helped me develop the most, and he's the one who was using the same development method as me. He is a strong believer that you should give your people big challenges, let them hit the wall, and then learn as they get back up. He's the one who taught me it's ok to fail as long as you learn from it. Why am I telling you this? If you want to use the same philosophy to develop your people, you need to make sure to create a safe environment where failure is accepted and it's not something one should be ashamed of. Furthermore, you need to ensure that you don't burn your people. While I do believe we develop the most when we have the most to do and when we are stretched, there's also a point when it becomes just too much.

YOU ARE RESPONSIBLE

The most important thing to have in mind, as we already touched on in Chapter 1, is that it's still your responsibility for that task or project you delegated to be completed. If your team member fails, you have failed. Now, that's a bit harsh, but it's your job, and it's your responsibility to enable your direct reports to perform. You're probably going to think, "But some people really cannot perform. I stepped in too many times for them and invested too much time to support them." Even if a team member doesn't perform, no matter how much you try, it's still your responsibility. Be honest with yourself: find another position or manage that person out. It's tough, but it's a price you pay when you are a manager.

"On any team, in any organization, all responsibility for success and failure rests with the leader. The leader must own everything in his or her world. There is no one else to blame. The leader must acknowledge mistakes and admit failures, take ownership of them, and develop a plan to win."

— *Extreme Ownership*

PROVIDE 100% SUPPORT

Whenever I'm giving my people tasks or projects, I always say they have free hands to do as they wish. Also, I tell them not to be afraid to try new things and go outside of their comfort zone. Even though I'm letting them act alone, I'm always there, and if they fail, I'll catch them before they hit the ground and help them get up again. This means creating a safe environment where employees are encouraged to try new approaches and where failure is accepted. Furthermore, the approach to development I preach requires a manager to devote a significant portion of their time to employees. If you really want to be a leader and grow your team, you need to be there for them, challenge them enough that they grow, and support them.

PART 4:
RETAIN

After hiring employees who are a great fit for the company and supporting them with development, the question comes as to how to retain them. My experience shows that motivated and engaged employees, with opportunities for continuous growth and development, are here to stay. However, that might not always be the case, and you should do what's best for the person. Let's slice it down even further.

01
HOW TO KEEP EMPLOYEES MOTIVATED?

"There's no such a thing as an unmotivated person, only an unmotivated employee. (...) Every single person on this planet has the ability to get excited and motivated about something. The leader's primary task is to get his team excited and motivated about the compelling cause that is his vision."

— *Robin Sharma*

I 100% agree with this statement. Each person has their interests, which are their fuel and energy to move on. It's on every leader to find out what that is and trigger it. I got to experience firsthand what this means and how powerful it can be. I got the pleasure of reporting to an extraordinary leader whom I learned a lot from. He was really tough and challenging. He would constantly add to my workload. Every week was a new challenge coming from him. I didn't mind it. I was happy and motivated because I was learning and growing. We had weekly 1:1s where we sometimes talked about most random things—travel experiences, books, etc. We would talk about business as well when there was something I needed his support with. After meeting with this manager, I had a feeling I could move mountains, like I could do anything and no challenge was too big for me. He knew how to motivate and engage me. He made sure that I followed his vision and understood the purpose behind what I was doing. I also had the opposite experience by reporting to a manager that quite often had a completely opposite effect. After 1:1s with that manager, I usually needed therapy sessions with my favorite coworkers. That manager was the first person that ever made me doubt myself. By nature, I'm a big believer, and I truly believe that anything is possible. I don't shy away from challenges, and I always think I can do it (within my field). If there's something new, something I don't know, I'll learn how to do it, and I'll make it; that has been my thinking for a long time. This manager succeeded in bringing me to a point where I was, for the first time, asking myself, "Am I capable of doing this? Will I succeed in that?" Now, this manager, like the previous one, wanted me to succeed, but he didn't know how to bring me along. He didn't know how to motivate me and keep me engaged. When he tried to challenge me, there was no purpose behind it, let alone encouragement, which left me doubting myself for the first time. Here, you have a true example of how to lead and how not to lead. Still, this was the case with me. Maybe other people would have a completely opposite reaction (which I highly doubt). The question remains: How do we keep people motivated? I'm going to share with you what I have discovered over the years in the hope it helps you.

BE GENUINELY INTERESTED

"Great follower-ship begins the day your people sense you truly have their best interests in mind. Only when they know you care about them as people will they go to the wall for you."

— *Robin Sharma*

I always invest time in understanding who my team members are as a people. I spend time learning about them, about their background, their interests, and hobbies, and who they are as a people. As explained in chapters before, I want to learn what their goals are and what drives them. I strongly believe that's important for establishing a relationship based on trust and mutual respect. You need to know who your people are beyond work. Trust me, your employees will appreciate that because you show interest and you care.

I spend a great deal of my time with people, sometimes just chatting over coffee. For example, I make sure to have an informal catchup with my direct reports every morning just to kick off the day. It's usually a conversation not related to work at all, just basic life stuff—How are they doing? How are the kids? etc. I'll grab them during the day, depending on the workload, just for a 15-minute coffee to check up on them, not in a way to ask what they are doing and give the whole business update, but rather how they are doing. Furthermore, I try to remember important happenings in their life and follow up on those. What I learned is that doing small things like asking about their wife's doctor appointment they talked about last week, how the house search is going, and whether the dog is better after being sick goes a long way. That kind of exchange is something I do weekly on 1:1s as well.

The point of the story is to show genuine interest in your people and show that you care. Show that you care about them as human beings, not just as people who came to perform certain tasks. Even though this has nothing to do with work, trust me, your employees' performance will be higher, they will be coming to work happier, and the work environment will be just more pleasant. There are managers who take the hard line and focus only on work. You might have different opinions, but I strongly disagree, and that's what my experience shows. We are all human beings, and we cannot always talk about work and only work.

INVOLVE YOUR PEOPLE

"The job of every leader is to define reality for his people."

— *Robin Sharma*

It is expected from every leader to come to his team with a great vision and a way forward. The leader's job is to set the North Star for their team and get them on board to follow that path. What I noticed is that it is difficult to sell a vision to your people if you just show them what you have come up with and where you want the team to go. People like to be involved, and people like to be asked for opinions along the way.

Storytime

When I took over a department in a former company, I sat with my direct reports, and we brainstormed together about where we wanted to take the department. Before coming to that meeting, I already had a vision, an idea where I saw the whole organization going forward. Had I just put this on the table, for sure, they would listen to me and would go on executing it. That would be more of a boss approach. Instead, I like to discuss my own ideas with the team before making any decision because they feel involved, and once they have this sense of ownership—then the idea is not only mine but also theirs—they own the execution and do it with full power. You could argue that you cannot always ask your team for input and that sometimes, decisions need to be made. I also made that point in earlier chapters, stating that democracy is sometimes overrated. However, here we are talking about the vision and way forward, and trust me, it's easier to do it this way. That doesn't mean you should give up on your idea if your team doesn't agree with it. It's all about how you present it and get their buy-in. Let me tell you about the time when, together with the team, we did something that seemed completely impossible to them. Taking over that department, we had the longest order processing time in the network of warehouses our company had, which was negatively impacting the time our customers had to wait longer for their packages to be delivered. We introduced system upgrades and decreased it down to acceptable levels. At that time, there was minimum automation across our departments, and leadership was happy with the time achieved. Going forward, my vision was to match the timings of fully automated fulfillment centers as I believed we could. I knew my team could do it, and by this, we would be significantly improving our customer experience. Since I remembered how they reacted to the first processing time decrease, I was expecting even bigger resistance with this. Instead of telling them, "Team, I want us to try this because...," I went naively and started asking questions. I asked questions like: What's the fastest time in which we can process orders? What can be our biggest problem when processing that fast? And after a short discussion, I just asked, "What do you think? Could we decrease our processing time further?" Since we already discussed what could be our fastest time, they were open to my question. They raised a few points, and the follow-up question was: What do we need to do to make it happen? They listed all actions, and as it appeared, they were all controllable by us. My next question was, "Do you think we can try it?" The answer was yes. We tried it with 15% of our packages for one week, leading to 100% within one month. Had I just come and told them, "This is my idea, let's do it," the resistance would have been enormous. They would try to do it, but just because I told them, not because they wanted to do it or they thought it was possible. Even before the meeting, I did calculations in my head, and I knew it was possible. I just needed their buy-in. I needed them to feel involved in making the decision and owning the execution. By asking the questions, I opened their minds. By asking for feedback, I got their buy-in, and it was implemented.

As managers, we cannot do anything without our team; they are the ones doing the job, and we need them for anything we want to do. The sooner you realize that, the easier it will be. By involving your team, not only will they jump on board and drive the execution, but they will feel motivated as well. You appreciate their opinion, you want to hear what they have to say, and they have the opportunity to be heard. They have the opportunity to make an impact. That's what drives motivation and engagement.

EXPLAIN THE PURPOSE

In the previous part, we have covered what you can do to bring your people on board and follow your vision or build jointly a vision. However, there will be moments when feedback from your team is welcomed, but it cannot impact the decision. The decision is there, and execution must happen. What to do then? Well, explain the purpose, the reason behind the decision, the why.

There is an excellent book by Simon Sinek called "Start with Why." While the book focuses on the overall meaning and purpose of the organization, it touches this level as well. The book gives a framework called Golden Circles, explaining how to approach selling a product to the customers or, in this case, an idea to employees. I'll sum up briefly the whole concept, but make sure to look it up or, even better, to read the whole book. The Golden Circles consist of Why, How, and What: WHY something needs to get done (the purpose), HOW it should be done, and at the end, WHAT needs to be done. When I'm giving a task to one of my team members, I start by explaining why; I always give an intro and a big picture. Then, I move on to giving the task by explaining what needs to be done and by when. If the task is not time-critical, I'll ask my team member to propose the timeline and offer the end date. And how the task needs to be done? Well, that part is up to them.

Not long ago, I was running a project, and I needed help from my team in data crunching. I asked my team for support. The support involved about two weeks of data analysis on thousands of our customer orders. They would need to spend approximately 1 to 2 hours daily along with their regular job on doing analytical work. Keep in mind that those are people who generally don't sit behind computers. Those are the operations guys who are on the floor making things happen with their team. What I was asking from them was completely out of what they usually do. I didn't just come and tell them, "Team, this needs to be done. You have two weeks' time." I sat with them and explained the whole project, what the ultimate goal is, and how their work will funnel into it. Basically, I gave them the reason behind it, I told them why, and I explained the purpose. The outcome of the project, which is very much based on the findings of the analysis, could have a significant improvement on the experience of our customers, which will lead to more sales. They all understood and worked diligently on it.

Let me share an additional example that had a much greater impact and involved my whole organization, which, at the time, was 80 people, not just my direct reports. My team was in charge of shipping all of our customer orders. The question that we as a management team had was how to ensure our team members are handling packages with care, as there is a high risk of damage when boxes are mishandled. It was easy to come and say, "Don't drop the box," but it would not have any effect. We again started by giving them purpose. We explained why we asked them to be careful: "Every box we ship is helping someone build a dream home. That box might be someone's children's bed, someone's dining table for the first home, etc." We gave them meaning that they are the ones who can make someone's experience of creating a home much more joyful. After constantly repeating and reminding our employees of the impact they have, we started noticing a reduction in damages reported by our customers.

Give people a purpose. Explain to them why their work matters and how they are influencing other people's lives. Help them understand what kind of impact their work has, and trust me, they will be motivated and engaged.

I have shared with you a few tips on how to keep your people motivated so that they come to work feeling engaged. This has so far worked for me and my teams. Keeping people motivated is a never-ending task, and over the years, I developed this approach, which is continuously evolving. I'm sure that on your leadership journey, you will figure out more initiatives that work for you and your team, but these are fundamental ones you should be doing.

DO YOU WANT TO MOTIVATE YOUR TEAM AND LEAD THEM TO A COMMON GOAL?

Show them you care.

Give them the reason, explain the purpose.

Involve them as soon as possible.

02
KEEP THE CHALLENGE HIGH

Previously, I wrote about how to keep the motivation and engagement of your team high, and I shared a few tips you should implement. However, when it comes to your talents and high performers, this is not enough. High potentials who are ambitious need to be constantly challenged and stretched. Those are the people who won't be happy if they are not developing and having new learnings. They are expecting exponential growth and development, and if you cannot provide them with that, they look for opportunities elsewhere. I myself was in a similar position not long ago.

The company I was working for offered me to step up into a stretch role, meaning I was keeping my current level but having responsibilities and tasks from the level above. For me, it was never about money; it was about development, growth, and learning. I took the opportunity. At the same time, the company was facing a downturn in demand for its products, sales declined, and expansion of the company was halted. During that time, I was never afraid for my position, but I started realizing that my drive and motivation for work were gone. Why? Due to the scaling back, work just became less fun, and there were not so many projects to take on and not many challenges. Even in that environment, the company decided to go with my official promotion to the next level. However, at the same time, I was reached out to by two different companies offering positions that would provide me with what I was missing—a challenge, a push outside of my comfort zone, exponential growth, and development. By the time my promotion was finalized, I was ready to sign with another company. My current company went above and beyond to offer a competitive compensation package, but that was not enough. I knew if I didn't take the step, I would not be happy, as I would still be in an environment where I was quite comfortable doing the same things as before. I decided to leave.

The point of the story is that with high potentials, offering titles and money will not count. Ambitious people who strive for continued growth like to be challenged, which is what keeps them motivated and engaged. Now, this could be interpreted very badly as I used myself as an example of a high potential, but let me have this one.

What do I usually do in these situations? It's mostly covered in the chapter before, development of the people. Usually, when people feel you are investing time in them, they see their continuous growth, they are challenged, and they will be engaged and motivated. A good example is one of the junior managers. He was offered the project manager position by his former manager in a new company. However, he declined. He declined a higher position, higher salary, and working for a company expanding much more than his current one. Why? His manager was continuously investing in his development. At that time, that person was given additional responsibilities and tasks, which kept his motivation and engagement high. In turn, he stayed at the company. This is just one example, and a lot of people would do so.

03
DON'T HOLD YOUR PEOPLE BACK

You have hired a great talent and invested hours and hours in developing the person, and you are wondering what you can do to ensure this person stays in your team and within the company? In today's world, it's quite normal that people are changing their roles, departments, and even companies frequently. This is especially true with talented high potentials. So the big question is, how to prevent them from leaving?

The answer for those managers who are afraid their direct reports might go to a different team or a role within the organization is simple: if the move will benefit your direct report and allow the person to develop even further, just support the move. No matter how hard it is, you should always put the interests of your people first and never block their development. The move will leave a gap in your team, and you'll lose one of your top performers? So be it. That's your problem, and you need to deal with it. If there are no growth opportunities, no projects, nothing you can challenge your direct report with that they will be content with, then support the move. You should not stop someone's development for your selfish reasons and the fact there's going to be "a hole" in your team. You'll end up with a highly disengaged person and be seen as a bad manager.

Storytime

I remember the situation not long ago. My colleague had just moved to a newly launched business unit, so I took over his team as well, along with other departments that we had integrated before. That meant I was doing a job previously done by three managers with eight direct reports. Let's just say my days were completely filled. My top performer and high potential also expressed the wish to move to the mentioned business unit. At that time, it was really a move that set back my part of the organization. I was highly reliant on that person; he was a person I could delegate a lot to, and he would deliver at the highest level. He was making great improvements in his area and was extremely self-driven and proactive, meaning there was not much for me to do apart from supporting him when needed. "Losing" him meant I was left with a huge gap in my team that I could not fill that easily. It really was a bad time for me to let that person go. However, I was aware I was not the one who made the decision; it was him. We had, and still have, a very good relationship. He expressed his wish and asked me for advice. Even though the decision was on him, I still could have made it very difficult for him to change departments, but I didn't. We had an open discussion, and I told him growth opportunities for him in my organization were limited in terms of promotion, and I was not sure when I would be able to go with that. I told him that if he wanted to have a faster trajectory to a higher level and do something new, he should move to a new business unit. Putting my interests aside, looking at the bigger picture, and supporting my direct report on his growth—that's what I decided to do.

Some managers don't understand that if your direct report wants to change departments, it's not your failure and it's not your loss. High potentials are always seeking new challenges and opportunities. If you cannot provide them with those, they will look elsewhere. That's normal. The most important thing is that it's not your decision; it's your direct report's decision. Your decision is to support their move or not, but they will leave regardless. In case I described, half a year down the road, I took a higher position and was looking for someone to take my former role. Naturally, I talked to this person, and he gladly accepted it. I was truly amazed by how much he grew in those six months. He was performing and behaving on a completely different level. By leaving my organization earlier and taking on a new role, he was put in situations and faced challenges he would not have had if he had stayed and would not have grown so fast. Seeing that just confirms I made a good decision by supporting his move. In the end, I didn't lose him, and we got to work together again.

The case I have described is when your direct report wants to make a change within the organization. But what to do if they want to leave the company completely? What to do and how to prevent it? Well, if that happens, and a person comes to you with a new offer, I usually don't discuss it and don't try to keep the person within the organization. If the person already went through the whole interview process with another company and got the offer, that means they are pretty serious about wanting to leave. There could be various factors for them wanting to leave, from personal to business-related. Private reasons are excluded, and there's, in general, not much that you could have done in the first place. Let's say it's a business-related reason, and a person was given a better opportunity to go to a higher position and face bigger challenges. What can you do apart from supporting the person? In case there is something you can do in terms of additional responsibilities, potential promotion, etc., well, the question is, why didn't you do it before? If you truly believed that person is capable of doing more, why didn't you give them more already? You should not try to stop someone from leaving by offering better "terms" just because you failed to do it in the first place. Happy and engaged employees who have bright prospects in the company won't even go into interviews with others. Long story short, if a person comes to you with an offer from another company, thank them for your contributions and support their way out.

I'm aware that the advice and answers I gave in this chapter probably don't work for small companies. I always worked in big companies with all the possible HR machinery you can imagine that will work hard to fill an empty role when an employee leaves. In that sense, I cannot relate to small companies and entrepreneurs, and probably my advice won't help. However, regardless of the size of the company you are coming from, one piece of advice that's applicable is you should always do your best so that your team members don't think about leaving. When a team member decides to go into discussions with another company and comes to you with an offer, it's already too late.

04
RECOGNISE

Too often, we are focused on getting things done and achieving our targets and goals. After that comes a new task on our list, and we pursue this one. It's a never-ending circle in which we get lost, constantly chasing the new thing we have to do, the new project, without celebrating the successes.

CELEBRATING SUCCESS

There is one really inspiring story I'll never forget. At the beginning of my career, I spent six months in Japan as a part of my management trainee program, which was an amazing experience in itself. There is one particular situation that has stuck in my head ever since. It was a Monday morning, and reports for last week's performance were just released. I remember the operations director and a board member of the business entering the open space office and coming directly to the delivery manager, who was his skip-level direct report. He told him in front of everyone how amazing a job he did last week as the performance of the delivery business had never been better and that he almost started jumping from happiness when he saw the cost-efficiency improvement. I was astonished by that move as never before had I witnessed a manager, let alone a director level, recognizing someone so openly and publicly with so many emotions.

I carry this memory with me ever since, as it was eye-opening for me, and I promised myself that I'd be a manager who doesn't shy away from recognizing his team members when they do succeed.

Reflecting, I don't think I'm doing it enough, and I know I need to work severely on improving that part of my leadership. I've been raised in a culture where recognition and rewards were rare, but when you got it, it meant you did an amazing job. My manager at that time was scarce on recognizing people verbally, but he was showing it in a different way. Afterward, I worked in a company where recognition of team members was strongly advocated and encouraged, sometimes even too much. At the beginning of every daily stand-up, we celebrated success stories from the day before and people who achieved those. Great idea, but our success stories dropped from "We successfully launched a building" to "We inbounded all items on time." In the absence of success stories, we started celebrating when someone did the job they were paid for. This is where my struggle with the topic of recognition and reward is coming from—a company where that culture is close to non-existent to a company where it's heavily overdone.

I would refrain from discussing rewards, as that heavily depends on the tools the company gives to you. As you can imagine, one company didn't give me many options to reward my team for great work, and the other offered a hefty budget and countless options. Let's rather discuss the recognition part, as that comes as free and depends solely on you and how you approach and treat your employees.

Recognizing someone for the good work they have done is essential for keeping engagement and motivation high. It keeps people going forward. It can be from a simple "thank you" to a praise speech in front of the whole team. The basic thing that must be done is saying thank you whenever you ask something from anyone. When you are a manager or even in a higher position, you will tell people to do something just because of the hierarchy, but that doesn't mean you should exploit it and just get on with it. Being nice and appreciative doesn't cost anything, but it makes a huge difference in how people feel. It's just a simple act of kindness that I have witnessed that's being missed too often. What I usually like to do is to circle back to the people once the task is done and thank them again for the great work or for helping out with something that was important.

The catch is also not to overdo it. Once, I had a manager who was thanking me for every single thing he asked me, which was completely over the top, and it didn't come out as trustworthy. It was appearing extremely fake, and I didn't like it. I'm a person who doesn't require constant petting on the shoulder, so as with everything else in a relationship with this manager, our approaches were misaligned. However, the point is that you need to be careful not to overdo it and make it count, make it trustworthy, and mean it when you say it.

To conclude, it's essential to recognize your people. I named a few ways to do it, and I'm 100% aware that's the area I really need to improve. No doubt. The endless fight I have is to give recognition but also to keep it meaningful. When you "overdo it," it just becomes a regular exchange, and people don't even notice it. As with everything in leadership, this is an art that each one of us has to master and find what works best for ourselves. For sure, there are universal guidelines, but each one of us needs to incorporate recognition and reward in our leadership style and do it the way it's authentic.

CELEBRATING PROGRESS

We discussed situations when your team achieves great success. However, there are many situations where the achievement isn't so big on a grand scale, but it's a very big step for a team member. Let's say you have a new team member, and it's normal that the person new in the role doesn't have a performance like a more experienced team member. It's expected that their performance will improve over time as they gain knowledge and experience. This is most visible when you source external candidates or promote someone within the organization. As mentioned before, those people will require a lot of your attention and time investment. You have for sure found yourself in the same situation, and you know how it feels; you're overwhelmed, sometimes lost, you want to do your best but don't know how, etc. The most important is that you cannot compare that person to your experienced team members and grade their output on the same level. Don't make that mistake. You need to watch out for how their development is going and whether the quality of their input is improving compared to what they produced before. Here, it's important to celebrate any wins. One of my skip-level team members was leading a weekly stand-up for the first time. He wanted to go to the next level. However, he lacked communication skills, a strong appearance, and exposure to large audiences. So, his direct manager encouraged him to take the chance and lead the meeting, which usually included the whole leadership team. The meeting was ok. We could see he was stressed and nervous. His voice was shaking, but he pulled it through. It was the first time he did it, and everyone appreciated it. Immediately after the meeting, I talked to him and thanked him for taking the challenge and for doing a great job! His reply was that he was not happy and that he didn't perform well.

Then I explained to him that this was his first time, and it's normal he's not satisfied and wants to improve, but he should also be proud of himself for making this step. Next time will only be better. In my view, that kind of encouragement is extremely important for people doing something for the first time. Often, there is the pressure that a person needs to do an amazing job, even when dealing with something completely new. Those expectations stress out the person even more. Here, I'm referring to people who are beginners or newcomers, excluding other situations.

There is a great reference to a child learning how to walk. When a child makes a few steps for the first time and then again continues to crawl, the parents will be super proud and happy. They will cheer the child for what they did, even though it was just a few steps. The same goes for new employees in your team; congratulate them and encourage them when they do something, no matter how insignificant overall it might seem. It could be a big step for them. I assume you would agree with me that a child learning to walk, overall, doesn't have a big impact. However, the closest ones are extremely proud.

You could say this chapter is filled with obvious behavior, and you are right. Most of the points here are basic human behavior and something everyone should practice in their daily lives regardless of their hierarchical level at work. Unfortunately, that's not the case, and hence, I decided to write about it, being fully aware this is one of my big opportunity areas and behavior I need to improve.

PART 5:
LAY OFF

Facing a situation in which you have to let go of someone is a difficult one, if not the worst. However, it's a part of the job, and any manager will, eventually, be in a position having to do that. I don't want to come out as ruthless, but it's the responsibility of any manager to manage out people who are not fit for the team, are not contributing, and the company is better off without. Over the years, I have had many of these situations, and I want to share with you a few points I learned. Those situations are unfortunate but inevitable and are also what builds a good leader and a people manager because making those decisions is not easy and takes a lot of courage to do it.

"If you can't part ways with someone, you are not a leader because that's an essential part of business."
— *Steffen Reckert*

01
WHEN IS IT TIME?

You have a low performer in your team. You already made a performance improvement plan with them, held plenty of feedback sessions, and offered them coaching, but nothing works? That means this person should probably not be on your team. You can keep trying, but you'll reach a point where time invested in that person is just lost, and they are consuming more time than your other reports. At that point, time invested is a huge opportunity cost as you could be supporting your high performers even more. The decision to let someone go is never easy, especially if a person is genuinely good and you care about them. However, you need to do what's best for your team and the company; by keeping low performers, you're doing exactly the opposite. Furthermore, you're risking losing the trust of your team. Your team will notice what's happening. You can be sure they'll be commenting behind your back on the performance of that individual. In the worst case, you'll turn out as an incompetent leader who's afraid to decide. Trust me, your team will appreciate you making a tough decision. One additional piece of advice: never keep a person who's not performing or is toxic just because you think you won't be able to replace them. I've seen managers do that, and situations only get worse. I witnessed a couple of managers admitting their direct reports were not fit for the position, but "Who else to get? It's better to at least have someone." The person in question was saying this repeatedly while doing nothing to improve the situation. That's completely wrong, and I have already discussed what can go wrong when you hold onto a person who shouldn't be in a position.

Storytime

Over the years, I faced many situations where I had to part ways with my team members. I'm supportive and always help—provide feedback, training, and support. However, if I don't see progress, there's only one way that can end up. The most recent case is a story I already started telling in the part of the difficult conversation; it's about Lucas. As mentioned earlier, we came to a point where he understood he was in the wrong position and there were no roles within the company, so he decided to look for opportunities outside. I was willing to give him the time. However, that took much longer than expected, and along the way, he became very toxic, spreading rumors and talking bad about the company. I decided he needed to go immediately. I aligned with HR, who prepared the documents, and we agreed on the strategy for the meeting. We literally agreed on who would start a meeting, say what, and in which sequence. It may seem like over-planning, but leading a meeting like that is never easy, and it's better to be well-prepared. I started the meeting by explaining the situation and why we were there, followed by my HR colleague explaining the options. Even though one could assume what would happen, Lucas was completely shocked and was not expecting this development. To this day, I still find it very strange he didn't see it coming. He took it very emotionally and even needed more than half an hour to get it together and make a decision. We provided him enough space to digest it and choose from two options offered (both of which meant it was his last day in the company). Was that conversation easy? Of course not! I felt personally very bad as he was a nice person with a family. However, my job was to protect the interests of the company and the well-being of my team. Having that person longer in this position was unacceptable. Even though the team was sad at the moment I shared the news, all of them understood and were more than aware of the reasons. The new manager took over the team, and performance immediately improved, and people were happier. Furthermore, it turned out quite well for this individual as well; he is working in an industry he loves, doing a job that fit his skills.

This is an example of a person who was just not fit for the role and, hence, had low performance. Furthermore, at the very end, even though they are generally nice people, they were a bit toxic. The much bigger problem is when you have a high performer who is toxic. What do I mean by toxic? That's a person bringing bad energy, disagreeing with everything leadership imposes, doesn't follow procedures, and consequently, has a bad influence on a team. No matter how good of a performer that person is, they need to go.

Storytime

I had that situation in the first team I was ever managing. The person in question was leading my inbound department, which is a huge responsibility. In the beginning, I had a lot of trust in him. The employee was exceptionally reliable, hardworking, diligent, and followed company procedures—at least the ones he liked. If he didn't like something, he wouldn't do it. As mentioned before, I had issues with confrontations at the beginning and was closing my eyes on misbehavior. However, at one point, I just could not tolerate it anymore. The more I requested the procedures to be followed, the more I was facing rejection. This didn't, however, influence the performance of the person; he was still hardworking. After repeated conversations and even warning letters, the situation didn't improve. However, hardworking or not, if company procedures and policies are deliberately broken, it's not acceptable. I was managing a store in the coastal part of Croatia, and this was happening during the summer, the busiest period when tourists from around the world flocked to our coast. I could not allow myself to lose anyone, but I could not keep going this way. After discussions with my manager and Human Resources, the decision was this person had to go right away, and that was what happened. The team was not happy, but again, they understood. Furthermore, this sent a strong message about doing what the company is requesting us to do.

This leads me to one other escape route some managers follow: transferring low performers to other departments. This is the way to go if you are sure the individual will perform better in a new department. In case the person isn't fit for the company, don't do it. It's your responsibility to take care of it and don't put your colleagues in bad situations where they have to deal with what you should have done in the first place.

You, as a manager, sometimes need to make a tough decision for the greater good—to protect your team or the company. No matter how hard it is, it's your responsibility and your job to do it. You need to take out the rotten fruit to save the healthy ones.

02
HOW TO DO IT?

How to let someone go? I'll share some advice on what I usually do. There is not a good way to let someone go. From what I have seen over the years, there are steps that can be taken in order to make it less painful for you and for the person in question.

NEVER DECIDE TO LET GO OF SOMEONE IF YOU HAVEN'T TRIED TO SUPPORT THEM

I have witnessed managers making snap decisions to release people without offering them support and helping them improve their performance. There are many tools you can use to support your direct report and letting them go should be your last choice once you have already tried everything else.

ASK FOR SUPPORT AND FEEDBACK

If you have peers you can discuss the case with, do it. They will give you their perspective of the situation and the person in question. You'll get feedback on your direct report which will be aligned with your thoughts or opposite. If it's the opposite, it means something else is a problem.

INVOLVE YOUR MANAGER AND HUMAN RESOURCES

As soon as you notice there might be a problem with one of your direct reports, mention this to your manager. Inform them of your action plan and that you will be monitoring it closely. Keep them updated. If the situation doesn't improve, inform Human Resources. Why is that important? First, you will get their feedback about the information. Second, if you need to let that person go, you'll have the backing of your key stakeholders, and they'll support you in executing. The last thing you need is to have to explain why you decided to proceed that way and justify your moves.

PREPARE YOURSELF

When the day comes and you need to convey the message to your direct report, it's not going to be easy. It never is. My advice is to prepare yourself in advance. Think about your storyline and practice it if necessary. Think about details, like your employee needs to pick up their stuff, give back company equipment, etc. Plan how it will go. The day will be difficult enough, and you don't need additional stress.

NEVER DO IT ALONE

Never ever have a meeting where you terminate someone alone; you always need to have a witness in those kinds of conversations. In case your employee decides to take legal action, you need to have someone confirm the story. The best is to always include Human Resources, as they can help if legal questions are asked. If not possible, ask your manager or peer.

DO IT FAST

The whole meeting will be painful. Make sure not to drag it; do it fast. You need to have an understanding that the person you're having this conversation with is going to be shocked and will need time to process it. However, be efficient.

BE EMPATHIC BUT NOT EMOTIONAL

It's normal that your heart will beat, and you will feel very uncomfortable. Furthermore, it's normal to be sad for the person, but don't show it too much. Keep your cool while delivering the message and refrain from long discussions but have understanding for a person who just lost the job.

FOLLOW THROUGH TILL THE END

In companies I have worked for, when a person is let go, they are usually released from duty immediately. When letting go of your direct report, after the paperwork is done, make sure to follow your employee to collect their stuff and escort them to the exit. It's horrible but necessary. I missed doing this once, and my direct report went on his goodbye crusade across the company, causing even more harm.

These are steps I usually follow when it's obvious a person has to leave. I encourage you to use this as a last resort when you tried everything and nothing worked, only when you are sure there's no other opportunity within the company for that person.

FINAL THOUGHTS

CONCLUSION

In the end, what is the difference between a boss and a leader? A leader is a person who creates a vision for his team and brings everyone on board to make it happen. That is someone who has a genuine interest in their people. They invest in their team members, in their development. Leaders also make tough decisions when needed, in the best interest of their team. And the boss, well, I guess you got the picture.

There is a saying that smart people learn from their mistakes and never make them twice. I fully agree, but I also agree with the addition that smart people learn from other people's mistakes. While I had amazing managers, colleagues, and team members I learned a lot from, there were also people who taught me how not to behave. Keep your eyes open and learn from bad examples and what not to do so you can avoid it with your teams. Learn from my mistakes as well. Also, don't be afraid. I know it can be frightening to be responsible for a team, no matter the size, and it can be overwhelming. Every story that I shared was a personal experience and a learning moment for me. Some of them were even "hitting the wall moments," where I fell, got back up, and learned from it. Use this book not to make the same mistakes I did, and if it happens, it's not the end of the world as long as you learn from it. Be curious, and be open to changes and challenges. Grab every opportunity and learn from it. You can learn a lot from your peers and your team members. Be open to that because you don't know everything, and as we established before, it's fine to admit it.

The ultimate goal behind writing this book is to help new managers in their first steps and challenges. I'm not a consultant or an HR professional, but everything I'm preaching and writing about in the book is based on my personal experience. The advice, rules, and tools I gave you are proven to work in real life. I've learned from my own mistakes, and I wish someone had given me structured knowledge about leadership at the beginning of my career, like in this book. I still have a lot to learn about leadership - I keep making mistakes and learning and improving. That's the circle of life in general, not just when it comes to the topic of leadership. However, I do hope advice, stories, and my personal learnings will help more people and make their people manager life easier.

THANK YOU

Many people have influenced my development and helped me come to where I am at the moment. It would be too much to mention all of them that left a footprint on my path. However, there are a few I'd like to particularly thank for their contribution to the development of my leadership skills and growth as a people manager.

First and special thanks go to Catalin and Marin, who were the inspiration behind this book. Your words and appreciation gave me the audacity to think I can write a book - and here it is.

I'd like to thank my two managers who left the biggest mark on my career and development, Tomislav and Steffen. Those are people whose leadership styles I always admired, and I learned a lot from them. I strongly believe my current leadership style, who I am as a manager, is very much influenced by them. They both invested a lot in my development and were tremendous support. I would not be where I am today without your guidance.

As mentioned in the book, at one point, I was the youngest manager in a company I worked for at that time. My success in that role, apart from Tomislav, I owe to my colleagues and dear friends Josipa and Mirela. Thank you for accepting me as a colleague on your level and for selflessly passing on your knowledge. Josipa, thank you for teaching me to lead from the heart. I'll never forget your words. Mirela, thank you for showing me how to lead by example and be tough at the same time. Baby Store Managers forever.

Even though we never worked together, thanks to one person who always calls me out when I'm not thinking big enough and always reminds me nothing is impossible, the one person who's never shying away from directing insults my way to push me into becoming a better version of myself. Thank you, Kristian.

Big thanks to the first readers of this book, who are, at the same time, great supporters and friends I can always count on—Alica and Petra.

Last but not least, a huge, huge thanks goes to my partners in crime, Marija and Dennis. "Chance made us colleagues. But the fun and laughter made us friends." Thank you for being my unpaid therapists, endless support, and my reality check.

AUTHOR BIOGRAPHY

Benjamin Babic, born in Croatia and now based in Germany, serves as the Logistics Director at Rathenower Optik, a production and logistics company within the Fielmann Group - leading eyewear company in Europe. He kickstarted his career in METRO Cash and Carry as a management trainee after obtaining a Master's Degree in Economics from the University of Zagreb in 2015. Benjamin quickly climbed the professional ladder, taking on his first managerial role as a Store Manager.

Having worked in both sales and operations, Benjamin decided to specialize in operations. In 2021, he made a move to Germany and joined Wayfair, a global e-commerce powerhouse, as an Operations Manager. Meanwhile, he completed the MBA program at the Frankfurt School of Finance and Management. Over time, Benjamin progressed to the role of Senior Manager, leading the order fulfillment department.

Beyond his expertise in operations and logistics, Benjamin sees himself as a people-centric manager and leader. He finds joy in collaborating with his teams and fostering their growth. Accumulating valuable leadership insights, Benjamin is passionate about sharing his knowledge with emerging leaders.

RESOURCES

- Babin, Leif and Willnick, Jocko. Extreme Ownership, St. Martins Press 2015
- Babin, Leif and Willnick, Jocko. The Dishotomy of Leadership, St. Martins Press 2018
- Blanchard, Ken. The One Minute Manager, Harper-Collins 2005
- Canfield, Jack. The Success Principles, Harper-Collins 2015
- Edmondson C., Amy. The Fearless Organization, John Wiley & Sons Inc., 2019
- Erikson, Thomas. Surrounded by Bad Bosses, St. Martins Essentials 2021
- Reckert, Steffen. Management meet Nietzche, Amazon Fulfilment 2023
- Sinek, Simon. Start with Why, Penguin 2011
- Sinek, Simon. Leaders Eat Last, Penguin 2017
- Sharma, Robin. Leadership Wisdom, Jaico Books 2022
- Welch, Jack. Winning, Harper 2007
- Zhuo, Julie. The Making of a Manager, Virgin Books 2019

ENDNOTES

[i] Folkman, Joseph and Zenger, Jack. Quiet Quitting Is About Bad Bosses, Not Bad Employees, HBR 2022.
(https://hbr.org/2022/08/quiet-quitting-is-about-bad-bosses-not-bad-employees)

[ii] Brower, Tracy. Managers Have Major Impact On Mental Health: How To Lead For Wellbeing, Forbes 2023
(https://www.forbes.com/sites/tracybrower/2023/01/29/managers-have-major-impact-on-mental-health-how-to-lead-for-wellbeing/?sh=1653ee482ec1)

[iii] DDI. New DDI Research: 57 Percent of Employees Quit Because of Their Boss, 2019 (https://www.prnewswire.com/news-releases/new-ddi-research-57-percent-of-employees-quit-because-of-their-boss-300971506.html)

[iv] Muthuraaman, Uma. Positional Power vs. Personal Power, TLEX Institute
(https://tlexinstitute.com/positional-power-vs-personal-power/#:~:text=Positional power is the authority,to maneuver or control others)

[v] Garvin, Lia. How to Stop Micromanaging and Start Empowering, HBR 2022
(https://hbr.org/2022/09/how-to-stop-micromanaging-and-start-empowering#:~:text=Micromanaging means being overly prescriptive,Annotate)

[vi] CIPD. Coaching and Mentoring, 2023
(https://www.cipd.org/en/knowledge/factsheets/coaching-mentoring-factsheet/)

[vii] Blanchard, Madeleine Homan. Manager, mentor or coach? Help! We need some distinctions! 2023 (https://www.chieflearningofficer.com/2023/06/13/manager-mentor-or-coach-help-we-need-some-distinctions/#:~:text=Managers%20can%20certainly%20mentor%20their,will%20often%20question%20your%20answers)

Printed in France by Amazon
Brétigny-sur-Orge, FR

16531418R00077